SPANISH ALPHABET

Travels from A to Z

John O'Neill

*'Like all travellers, I have seen more than I remember, and I remember
more than I have seen.'*
Benjamin Disraeli.

*'I see my path but I don't know where it leads. Not knowing where I'm
going is what inspires me to travel.'*
Rosalía de Castro, Galician Poet, 1837-1885

ISBN: 978-1-4716-3555-7

JOHN O'NEILL was born in the south end of Liverpool, where he was educated at Holy Trinity Junior School, before going on to De La Salle Grammar School in 1956. In 1963-1966 he studied at Liverpool and Coimbra (Portugal) Universities, where, after three wonderful years, he graduated from the School of Hispanic Studies.

He was fortunate enough to teach Spanish for thirty-nine years, the last twenty-seven in Saint Mary's College, Great Crosby, of which he has determined to have nothing but the fondest memories, of which there were many.

He and Margaret moved to Galicia in Spain's north-west in 2006, where they live within a stone's throw of Catherine and Simon, Iman and Arantxa, and the beloved grandchildren, Ángela, Cael and Mia, angels every one of them.

He is the author of "Of Castles and Caballeros: Travels in lesser known Spain" (2010), and "Under The Bridge: Memories of a Garston Childhood" (2011).

My thanks to Margaret, who read the manuscript and told me what to leave out, and to Catherine, who, for the third time in two years, somehow managed to find the time to put it all together.

For Elizabeth and James O'Neill,

Margaret,

Ángela and Cael and Mia,

Catherine and Iman, Arantxa and Simon.

For : BERNADETTE
and PAUL.

Tourón,
August 2012.

CONTENTS

1. Three for the price of one!

The whole point and focus of the present book was to travel around Spain from A to Z, describing a single town or city or village – preferably generally little known to most English readers – for each of the 27 letters of the Spanish alphabet, to record personal observations and potentially contentious opinions (which, some will say, is my forte!).

I have to tell you, Reader, that I've fallen at the very first hurdle! But since I'm The Author – ahem! – I'll give myself some latitude on this one occasion, the more so since Almagro, Astudillo and Ayllón, in no particular order, are all in their way (perhaps not equally) worthy of mention and description. To choose one over the other, to eliminate two of them on this occasion, can hardly be to your potential advantage, the more so since (hopefully!) I've whetted your appetite. How's that for bending self made rules and justifying a measure of incompetence!

(Believe me when I tell you I could have usefully included Aguilar de Campóo, where we broke our journey from Reinosa to the banks of the Pisuerga with forty odd kids – some of them very odd – with The Lovely Sue and Wigan John, on our way to find better weather when it turned nasty in coastal Comillas. Or Atienza and its dominating ruined castle where Alan yet again insisted on going down into the dungeons – "I know me way! I'm an engineer, you know!" – Barbara hopelessly shaking her head in disbelief at his misplaced youthful antics.)

But the only reason we stopped at Ayllón that first time was that the 350 kilometres from Terrific Toro to Siguenza's stunning parador is a whole lot longer than it appears on the very best of maps, I can assure you. It looks pretty easy, in fact: Toro to Tordesillas, shaving the southern end of Valladolid and onwards in an easterly direction through Aranda del Duero (there's another 'A' for you!), south-easterly on a jinking little back road called – the last time we travelled it – the SG-945, winding on and on and on along something called the CL 110, past the aforementioned Atienza, and on to Siguenza. What could be easier?

Bernadette and Paul in the back of the car were justifiably showing the very earliest stages of well masked discomfort, it was wet and windy, and, more to the point, coffee had not been consumed since breakfast in Toro, and was now just a nagging memory. The second time we went, with Pauline and snap-happy Henry, the weather was glorious. So was Ayllón.

It's less than one hundred miles north of Madrid, but socially and culturally it's far more; and it's in the north east of the varied province of Segovia, on the borders of Machado's bitter-sweet Soria, where he loved and quietly lost his adored, teenaged Leonor.

Its Main Square, such as it is, is slightly irregular, more or less the shape of a parallelogram, porticoes on all four sides, and was made to be used. Medieval Market Day, a big event in this neck of the woods, is the last weekend in July, though there's a bi-monthly market held there, too.

Kings and queens too numerous to mention have passed this way, tarried a while for a bite and a wee, and have moved on. Even the great El Cid – alias Charlton Heston – passed through, fighting either infidels or Christian kings, depending on the identity of his current employer and paymaster. God's Nomad, Saint Teresa of Ávila, was also here, on God's business, of course, and even Italian Francis of Assisi graced Ayllón with his presence, founding the (now ruined) convent of Saint Francis in 1214.

One of the countless treaties between Spain and Portugal was signed in this relatively insignificant little town, this one in 1411 during the lengthy reign of the hesitant Juan II, who unknowingly gave his name to Terrific Toro's best hotel. Juan himself, by common consent, was a bit of a jessie and something of a coward (but we won't dwell on that at this stage of the game).

Ayllón's got a Roman bridge over the River Aguisejo and still boasts a section of its medieval walls and the imposing El Arco Puerta de San Juan, principal entry into the old town. The Town Hall is beautifully renovated in its original form, whilst behind it rears up the Church of Santa María La Mayor. That, and the twelfth century Church of San Miguel, Ayllón's patron saint, will repay time and attention.

But it's the ambience and the 'feel' of a place like this – as in a multitude of small (largely unknown) towns scattered throughout Spain, which has more to do with the experiences had and the people seen – that's

3

the greatest attraction, rather than, necessarily, with any single monument or monumental setting.

And 'diestro Alilon' (to quote from 'El Cantar de Mío Cid') has got this 'feel' aplenty. Every church, every run-down and dilapidated palace with its coat of arms, every street and street corner is an original film set authentically lifted from medieval times. Meanwhile, the relatively close-by A1 (called the N110 in some maps, just to complicate things!) barrels its way south to Madrid, a million cultural miles away, northerly towards isolated Soria.

On all our visits we've stopped for a bite to eat and entered the wonderful cacophony of noise and sound which Spaniards do so well (and which seems so perfectly natural, so that Portugal's almost silent bars and restaurants seem distinctly unnatural). The locals look at you – nay, stare at you – with that natural, innocent curiosity all Spaniards seem to have, not an ounce of hostility or unfriendliness in their stares. Waitresses scurry about and effortlessly commit to memory every item of your order, parrying sexual remarks with total aplomb, silencing the would-be Tenorio with a well chosen insult or a withering glance. People at the next table move their table to accommodate the four of us (and Alan's endless legs and size thirteen feet splayed out in front of him) assuring us there's not the slightest problem. We're greeted by complete strangers, who realise we're outsiders, and they encourage us to enjoy our meal. Being English, we smile in embarrassed fashion.

Even a noisy group of hairy bikers, their leathers and helmets and drinks piled high on a neighbouring table, greet us with a slight lifting of the chin and remove their accumulated wardrobe without the slightest hesitation.

(Why is it, by the way, that bikers the world over dress – if 'dress' is the correct word – the way they do? Long hair, apparently unwashed in recent months, unshaven faces, tattooed flesh, elephant-arse leather trousers, cutaway and torn leather jackets. And the male of the species don't look too good, either.)

But there's no malice in them, no menace, and they're sensible and wise enough to want to spend their Sundays here, wherever they come from, and we applaud their choice. And so are we, and not just Sundays, either. Ayllón's just a lovely place to be.

Now, much maligned and seldom visited Palencia province is to the north of Madrid, and the province's capital, as you will have guessed, is painfully, embarrassingly modest Palencia. But just a bare thirty kilometres outside of the capital, in a north-easterly direction, is the unassuming little town of Astudillo.

You go through gently undulating fields upon fields upon fields of waving wheat and fallow expanses in this (quite possibly) flattest part of mountainous Spain, and there, out of the blue, as it were, appears Astudillo.

Believe it or not, Reader, and I'm sure you will, I've not only been to Astudillo but I have the t-shirt to prove it. Tastefully embroidered on my left breast is the inscription, 'De Astudillo Sale el Sol' (The sun shines out of Astudillo), which is a very brave thing to say about such a largely unknown place, when you come to think of it.

It's a sort of fading red – the t-shirt, not the small town of Astudillo – but I still wear it with no small amount of pride as it invites myopic stares. Cael finds it utterly fascinating. Still, Cael finds almost everything utterly fascinating. I once had a navy blue t-shirt with the same crest. Cael barfed on it once too often, so it was reluctantly deemed beyond its sell-by date for public appearances, ending its days as a gardening garment. But since Cael is a beauty boy, we'll make no further comment, since he's also very sensitive, in spite of possible appearances to the contrary.

The first time we went to Astudillo (with Bernadette and Paul: yes, here they are again, in the vanguard of adventure) we stopped there on a whim, and because we were hungry yet again (and probably needed a wee, again). We parked just yards (or metres, if you prefer) off the modest town square, near the Tourist Information Office, where, incidentally, I bought the t-shirts, to the boundless joy of the three people behind the counter. We espied the somewhat dilapidated façade of a 'mesón', went inside, almost toppling down the steps into the gloom of a small bar and sitting area which can't have changed all that much since Cervantes was a lad.

Massive – truly, truly massive – roughly cut beams supported by equally massive trunks of (barely planed) wood; two rough tables, which were entirely functional and probably medieval; benches of the same ilk; monster barrels of the local brew, floor to ceiling; half a dozen local yokels used to the gloom, drinking and talking noisily and all at the same time in the manner expected of all full-blooded Spanish yokels, clearing their throats noisily and expectorating accurately.

A teenaged girl with attitude and a face like a smacked arse served us a board – and I do mean a board, the size of a small door – of cold meats and cheeses, a Dumpster full of bread, and a bottle of the local red, no label on it, of course. It was a veritable feast and we ate everything in sight. Briefly, after the second bottle, we saw the waitress in a new light, in spite of the gloom.

By the time we finished and left a tip, which failed to effect much change in her manner, it was almost five o'clock. In spite of the heat, we decided to walk around the town in what passed for a spasm of gentle exercise. Paul and I left the ladies to their own devices and they immediately copped off with an octogenarian peasant who offered to show them his underground 'bodega'. They genteelly declined: they didn't say why.

With minor changes and slightly different characteristics, Astudillo is like a hundred and one other Spanish towns of similar size. Go and find your own, Reader. You'll be well rewarded, believe me. Then come back and tell us your adventures.

In 1960, the population of Astudillo was almost twice its present twelve hundred souls; and the decline, both before and since, is symptomatic of much of rural Spain, where machines have sidelined manpower, and successive generations have gravitated to bigger cities (even Palencia!) in search of work and a different way of life. A return to former levels of population is quite clearly beyond expectations. The results, most especially in Castilla-León and Castilla-La Mancha (and north-westerly Galicia), are innumerable villages with little vestige of human habitation.

For all that, however, Astudillo (amongst many similar towns) is more than worth your time. It's a place full of back streets at all angles, with old houses being tastefully renovated – thank God somebody cares! – and its ordinary-looking town square is still the centre of social intercourse.

The lady in the tourist office, learning that Margaret was 'rather keen' on all things Greek and Roman, confessed that she, too, was a Classics graduate (from the University of Valladolid), and they talked excitedly about their common interests and obsessions. She gave them (Bernadette went, too) an impromptu guided tour of the Ruta de Las Bodegas, from which all three returned in a happy state of mind and smiling inanely, though walking slightly wobbly.

She was keen, she told them, for the authorities to spend some money to refurbish centuries' old buildings of worth in the town, but she confessed that that was unlikely to happen.

"Of course, the Poor Clares, they get everything they want from the authorities to rebuild their places! We don't!" Make of that remark what you will. I'm saying nowt.

So, we went to the Poor Clares' convent, five minutes' walk from the Main Square, and arrived just as they were opening the convent's museum, now housed in the Palace of Peter the Cruel.

Now, Peter – officially Peter I, though seldom if ever so referred to by history – came to the throne at the tender age of fifteen, a savagely ambitious young feller, and the eldest of five illegitimate brothers. To his friends and cronies he was known as the Dispenser of Justice, but, in effect, he was what we'd now call a serial murderer, comfortably in the Sadam and Ghadaffi and Assad class.

It's commonly accepted by historians that he personally murdered one archbishop, numerous cousins, a couple of brothers, and countless friends – friends! Ha! – in the course of his almost twenty year reign in the mid fourteenth century. And there's every indication that his French wife didn't die of natural causes, either.

To maintain his position, Powerful Pete was aided by no less a person than The Black Prince in his ongoing fight with his half-brother, Enrique de Trastámara. Known, not unnaturally, as Enrique the Bastard, he had the last laugh, so to speak, stabbing Peter to death in a tent. So much for romance, chivalry, and half-brotherly love!

(Chaucer, by the way, in his 'Monk's Tale', refers to Peter as 'O noble, O worthy Petro, glorie of Spagne! Whom Fortune heeld so hye in magestee!' Oh, come off it, Geoff! Don't be so bloody daft!)

But the museum was nice. Or it would have been if the elderly nun, who was our guide and who walked in a lopsided manner which invariably led to a collision with some artefact or other, had not herself been overcome by the presence in the group of a formerly famous sportsman. We never did work out which particular sport he had once excelled in, but the small group of three portly Basques were very friendly (something we didn't expect from Basques, I have to say).

Here's another thing. If you manage to be in Astudillo at precisely five minutes past four on 17 September, you'll witness the local version of the Bull Run. Dozens and dozens of youngsters, and grown men who should surely know better, but don't, tether a 500 kilogram bull (that's over a thousand pounds, by the way; eighty stone!) to the side of a building prior to letting it loose around the streets. Some of the buildings have never recovered, to say nothing of some youngsters and grown men (who should surely know better, but who, I repeat, don't).

Oh, what fun unconfined is had by one and all! But, seriously, somebody's got to take me aside and quietly explain to me in a manner my cretinous brain will accept what exactly is the fun in such an event. I'm not being awkward, but, honest to God, I'm culturally unmoved!

Anyway, undeterred, we got in some token exercise of our own in preparation for dinner. We meandered down to the Pisuerga.

Now the Ebro and the Tagus and the Duero, maybe even the southerly sited Guadalquivir and Guadiana, you'll have heard of, Reader. But the Pisuerga? Never! Yet this belting, unostentatious little river, that knows its place and does its job without fuss or fanfare, is only 40 kilometres short of Machado's mighty Duero, which the Pisuerga joins near Simancas (translation of Simancas: Seven One Armed Women. Honestly!). The Pisuerga even burst its banks in 2001 on its way through Valladolid, so there! Three hearty cheers for the plucky Pisuerga!

Final word on Astudillo: The Book (Shock! Horror!) doesn't even mention it! Do not, never for an instance, let this put you off seeing Astudillo. As to The Book – well, I'm beginning to see how it could be improved. Words will have to be had, I can assure you!

And then there's Almagro. If I'd left it out, Barbara would never speak to me again, so let me tell you a thing or two about it. Well, it's named in honour of Diego de Almagro, who once upon a time ruled Chile on behalf of the Spanish Crown (and made a mint for himself, whilst he was at it). So I suppose you'd have to say he made something of himself all those 400-odd years ago. Not unexpectedly, his statue commands the other end of the Main Square to the Tourist Information Office.

Before him, this town of nine thousand lucky inhabitants rose to immense prominence in medieval times when the warrior Order of The Knights of Calatrava, Spain's first of the many military orders, made it their base, thus bringing fame and no small amount of fortune to Almagro. And in many towns in present day Castilla-La Mancha (once known as New Castile, or Castilla La Nueva), it was once upon a time and for almost eight hundred years something of a bulwark against the ever encroaching and frequently changing Muslim frontier.

We first went there, Margaret and I, in July, 1990, passing through on the way to Madrid after dropping Simon off in southern, summer-steaming Úbeda. We got to Almagro in the middle of the afternoon, and were frankly a bit disappointed. The town seemed to be doubling up as a morgue. Here and there, a tired barman mechanically served a few heat dazed tourists, and in the Mesón del Gordo, The Fat Man moved from table to table in a slovenly, sluggish manner, his mind not at all on his job. The dogs sought the shade and counted their fleas, the natives were all indoors behind shuttered windows, so we went back to our less than appetising hotel on the edge of town and grunted ourselves to sleep.

Our second visit, some fifteen or more years later, scandalously treated Almagro yet again as a stop-over for lunch, after which we sat in the marvellous Plaza Mayor and people-watched. We were headed for somewhere called Villanueva de los Infantes and thence to Zafra. Barbara put on her best pout, truculently asked why we weren't spending at least one night in Almagro, wondered aloud what Villanueva de los Infantes could possibly have in the way of improvement, and quietly made it clear that our friendship was on a tightrope. Alan looked on, apparently with no opinion on the matter, or, maybe, careful to be impartial.

Finally, in 2010, we actually stayed there for two whole days and nights, no less, in the enormously beautiful parador, once the Franciscan Convent of Santa Catalina (in February's rain, which flooded the whole of central and southern Spain, rivers overflowing left, right and centre, Barbara not at all impressed with this manifestation of Sunny Spain).

There are churches galore: The Mother of God, Saint Blaise, the Convent Church of Our Lady of the Holy Rosary, the Convent Church of the Most Holy Sacrament, the Church of the Annunciation, the Church of the Incarnation, the Jesuit Church of San Bartolomé, the Church of The Assumption (and that's only for starters, to give you a flavour, so to speak).

There's the National Museum of Classical Theatre; the Museum of Embroidery, over which Barbara drooled and from which she had to be physically dragged; a Museum of Contemporary Art; a grand house that once belonged to Philip II's Fuggers, who did their little bit to bankrupt sixteenth century Spain, making a personal packet on the side, as you might expect. Thereafter, they were known as 'Them Fuggers', whenever anything went wrong, or when Spaniards needed a scapegoat (as in: "It wasn't me, it was Them Fuggers over there").

And there's the quite superbly atmospheric Corral de Las Comedias in the Main Square, built in 1628 and lovingly restored and maintained. It was here that Lope de Vega's famous dramas were performed: El Caballero de Olmedo, Fuenteovejuna, Peribáñez, and legions more (which we ploughed through at university and found mildly amusing). Reputedly he wrote eighteen hundred such plays, of which almost five hundred survive. And he wrote masses of poetry. That's a fact. Shakespeare wrote thirty seven plays. And that's a fact, too.

And then there's the Main Square, the 'Plaza Mayor'. It's a veritable stunner. With porticoes on two parallel sides, open at its two shorter ends, its wood painted a pleasing shade of green (like my twelve-stringed guitar), it's about the size of a football pitch, and it's simply a lovely place to spend the day. Under the porticoes are bars and gift shops and lace shops and gift shops and bars and endless knicker shops.

But tear yourself away from the Plaza Mayor, however briefly, and get lost down narrow, whitewashed streets with more than a hint to them of southerly Andalucía. Hear the noises and smell the smells and close your eyes and stand still and recreate what Almagro must have been like centuries ago, and enjoy the dream. It's what we four did for two whole days in February 2010, in spite of the inclement weather.

It was down one of these backstreets (Calle de Chile, actually) that Margaret stopped in front of a renovated façade which shared walls on both sides with two houses in ruins. It's the Museum of Mankind (Museo Etnográfico) and it's privately owned by a Biology teacher in his early sixties who lives across the street from it.

Entirely at his own expense, he has managed to renovate more than a dozen rooms of varying sizes and fill them with tools and utensils and everything you could possibly think of associated with more than a dozen trades, each one having a different theme: baker, wheelwright, farrier, hosier, carpenter, and many more. We had two wonderful hours of a social history lesson there, and Alan, who's fearless and fluid in Spanglish, had to be dragged out at the end. He's fixated with tools. He's got a shed-full back in flat Formby.

But I'll personally remember Almagro for a much more mundane reason. Leaving westerly Plasencia's parador three days previously, I'd managed with consummate ease to scrape the hire car in the parador's lift – yes, Reader, a car lift! – and a hefty bill would be the outcome. On the journey across via Cáceres and Trujillo and Guadalupe in Spain's achingly beautiful region of Extremadura, the inevitable loss of the heavy deposit, all eight hundred euros, weighed heavily on my mind. I recall doing a lot of swearing and meandering monologues.

Alan counselled against doing anything in the hope that the hire car people in Barajas wouldn't notice – honestly! A bloody big gash a metre long and they wouldn't notice! – rather than getting some Spanish mechanic to make a further mess of it. There's still this misplaced belief in some quarters that British is best. ("You can't trust these fellers", he commented authoritatively.)

Taking the bull by the horns – one of my Father's favourite phrases, though he never once did anything really adventurous in his life, God bless him – I explained my predicament to the nice man at the reception desk in Almagro's parador.

No problem, he assured me quietly. Didn't he just know the very man who could fix it better than new! Having no alternative, opting to make the decision myself and bear the financial consequences in the (largely mistaken) belief that 'it would teach me a lesson', I drove the car around the one way system for twenty minutes and more in a persistent drizzle, eventually finding the garage in the Ronda de San Francisco, little more than one hundred metres from the parador. That's me, The Great Navigator! Jesus!

The man was a veritable artist, right up there with the likes of Velázquez, El Greco, Zurbarán and Murillo. Self consciously he asked me if I thought his quotation of one hundred euros was too much. As if! And the very least I can do is to tell you that his name is Sánchez, and that his workshop is in the Ronda de San Francisco, number 8, post code 13270, Almagro (Province of Ciudad Real). Tell him that an inordinately grateful Englishman of a certain age and vacant look in his eyes remembers him with immense affection, and don't hesitate to give him your business (the next time you prang a hire car coming out of the car lift in Plasencia's parador).

(P.S. Here's one for your notebook to trot out at some swish dinner party or Pub Quiz and impress your friends: Almagro, along with its countless qualities, is the aubergine capital of Spain! Now, then!)

2. Two Catholic priests, a dog, and Baiona

This much is verifiably true. On 3 August, 1492, the three sailing ships, 'Pinta', 'Niña' and 'Santa María', under the overall command of Cristóbal Colón (Christopher Columbus, to most of us), and nobly assisted by the Ponzón Brothers, left the Spanish south-west port of Palos de la Frontera, in the province of distant Huelva, Andalucía, in Spain's deepest south.

After signing on for the voyage (of indefinite duration) and generally getting to know each other, they spent one month in the Canary Islands, refitting, repairing and replenishing the vessels, waiting for favourable winds, and having quite a nice time in the sun, thank you very much. It was September, the weather was extremely pleasant down in west Andalucía, and the lads were off on the adventure of a lifetime, looking for Cipango (Japan) in search of fame and fortune. The fact that they were going in completely the wrong direction didn't seem to bother them overly much at the time. They were content, at this stage of the venture, to leave that sort of decision to Chris. And, of course, they didn't know they were going in the wrong direction (and he didn't tell them when the truth eventually dawned on him).

But for the next thirty-six days or so, cooped up in ships not much bigger than a tennis court, sloshed and battered hither and yon on the merciless Atlantic, they encountered nothing but trouble, and were extremely bothered, to say the least, by the way things were turning out: this wasn't what they'd signed up for, after all. So unsure was he of just exactly where they were, and with the lads justifiably miffed because they didn't know where they were, either, Columbus falsified the logs on a daily basis in an effort to pacify them: "Not far now, lads, any day now, just over the next horizon", but there was, as they say, a whiff of mutiny in the air. So, when a bleary-eyed and painfully sunburnt lookout croaked the immortal, longed for cry of 'Land ahoy!' Chris heaved a sigh of relief for the first time in five very long, very trying weeks, changed his under-crackers for the first time in a few weeks, and thus forestalled an almost certain mutiny.

After they had established themselves on the most basic level in their newly found surroundings, it was decided that the 'Pinta' and the 'Niña' should set a course for Spain on 16 January, 1493, to tell the folks back home, and their royal backers, Fernando and Isabel, the celebrated 'Reyes

Católicos', where they'd been and what they'd seen and found. The 'Santa María' was left behind: engine trouble, or something.

(Excuse me, Author, do you think I might have a word? Now, you'll correct me if I'm wrong, but I was under the distinct impression that this was 'B for Barcelona', or perhaps even 'B for Bilbao'. 'B' for anything beginning with a 'B' would be fine at this stage: take your pick. Unless I've missed something here or wasn't paying attention, none of the places so far mentioned, like Huelva and Palos de la Frontera, begins with the letter 'B'. Care to explain?)

As I was saying: the two ships got caught in the mother and father of Atlantic storms on 14 February, a month into their return journey. The 'Niña' was blown southerly into Lisbon harbour, for which it was inordinately grateful, whilst the 'Pinta' eventually made landfall two very long and trying weeks later on the first day of March, many hundreds of kilometres further north in Bayona: 'B for Bayona' (or Baiona, if you like, in the Galician dialect). See the connection now, then?

God knows what Martín Alonso Pinzón's first impression of Baiona was. But when Father John Gerard Feeney, accompanied by his trusty dog and Father Fat Pete, first laid eyes on Baiona, he thought he'd taken a wrong turning (like Columbus, more than five hundred years previously) and was in the south of France, Father John being a connoisseur of most things French, and most especially its food and wines and camp sites. Pete and dog, too. His initial confusion had nothing to do with the fact that Bayona and Bayonne bear more than a passing similarity in their written form. It's just that Spanish Bayona was not what he'd actually expected of Spain (namely, in no particular order, guitars and flamenco; ravishingly beautiful señoritas with roses between their teeth and behind their ears; matadors in painfully tight trousers, wincing as they walked, pirouetting on their tippy-toes and killing bloody big bulls; civil guards with their funny plastic hats; a dictator called Franco, now thirty-five years dead and largely forgotten; a population with a deep commitment to their Catholic Faith (ha!); pungently smelling cigars, chorizo, and remarkably fine wines, and plenty of the latter, if you please, barman).

But, if you want to see Baiona at its best, come down the AP 9 from northerly Santiago de Compostela – which the two Catholic priests (and a dog) had surely visited in their travels, them being Catholic priests, and all that – pass sprawling Vigo on your right, thank God it's not on your itinerary, and veer onto the under-used AG-57 toll road. Some five kilometres or so before you actually arrive in Baiona, coming in from the western end, you'll have extensive panoramic views of the small town and its enchanting, picturesque bay.

When you get to the end of the AG-57, turn right at the roundabout and follow the coast road until you shortly see the turn off to the left to the Monte Boi peninsula and the impressively clean-cut Parador Nacional Conde de Gondomar, built on an eminence. Lovely place.

Behind you, the rocky beaches of Os Frades and Concheira; to your left, the wild Atlantic (pretty placid in this early summer of 2010); immediately below and in front of you, the smaller beaches of Barbeira and Ribeira, and the whole beautiful Ría de Baiona, swinging around in a graceful arc, Nigrán on the other side of the bay, shimmering in the heat haze.

Park the car – or, in John's case, the immensely comfortable mobile home – let the dog out, sit on the terrace of the Parador, get FFP to order 'cafés cortados', or, preferably, something stronger, to celebrate your arrival, and look over the balustrade towards Baiona and its harbour, delightfully spread out before you.

Immediately in front of you is the small, impeccably clean Barbeira Beach, and further along, to your right, the rather swish Club de Yates de

Monterreal. Further still, there's a replica of the famous 'Pinta'. Pay the euro to go on board, and let your imagination lose itself in thoughts of what it really must have been like to cross the fearsome Atlantic five hundred years ago in this tiny craft (even if its beams are sturdy and correctly weathered). The guide, himself a sailor of many years, told us sheepishly that he and half a dozen other maritime chums actually once sailed the caravel around the peninsular and out to the Islas Cíes, and every one of them was unspeakably seasick.

Beyond that, hundreds of crafts, from Abramovich-type, horrendously expensive yachts to one-man rowing boats, fill the Puerto Deportivo, none of which should come as a surprise, since Baiona is a sea-port, historically and inseparably wedded to the sea. It still sends commercial fishing boats way out into the Atlantic in all weathers in search of goodies for the countless restaurants in the town.

But, essentially, Tourism is King – even if the Tourist Information Office has been housed in a portacabin for the last ten years or so (surely not acceptable!) – and this small town of some twelve thousand quadruples during the summer, even in these economically fraught times. Incidentally, has there ever been in history an extended period of time in which the economy (national or otherwise, of any country, not just Spain) has never been other than fraught? Answers on a postcard, please.

Yet, except for the closure of one or two shops on the front, if you sit and people-watch the crowds inside and outside the bars and restaurants, you'd never think these were, yet again, parlous economic times. Step into any one of the numerous side streets into the old quarter, the 'casco histórico', with its centuries' old buildings which could tell a tale or two, and it's like a human beehive of locals and day trippers and summer residents, crowding the narrow, stone-paved streets, loud and good-natured and spending money as if they were Greeks and had millions belonging to others to throw around.

Back on the promenade, the Calle Elduayen Alférez Barreiro, shop fronts and flats are architecturally attractive in a simple, understated way. Get to the Puerto Deportivo, where the very same street, for some reason, now becomes Avenida de Monterreal, and the three and four story flats are art deco and uniformly ugly and out of place, quite a few of them offering two-month occupancy for the summer months to out-of-towners with money to burn.

But, that apart, you'll be thrilled with Baiona with its easy mix of the (relatively) formal and its wonderfully welcoming familiarity, its million dollar yachts and its rowing boats, its varied restaurants and bars. John and dog and FFP liked it, even if their one week stay in August in the excellent Camping Baiona Playa lasted one single night, when they found their pitch was next to the chemical toilets. No prize for guessing where they ended up, is there ... Try 'a little village in the mountains, a dozen kilometres or so east-south-east of Pontevedra, in sight of the PO-532 and just short of Ponte Caldelas' ... Got it?

3. Looking for John

We got to La Carolina towards midday and went straight to the main square where we parked in full sunlight and what must have been near zero temperatures. It was intended as nothing more than a pit-stop: a coffee, perhaps, and a wee, and then we'd push off in a northerly direction towards Madrid, maybe stopping the night in Chinchón before catching the Easyjet from Barajas Airport to Liverpool the following afternoon.

La Carolina just about qualifies as being part of that enormous southern wedge of Spain that's Andalucía, located as it is almost on the southern border with the rolling plains of Don Quijote's Castilla-La Mancha, with which, scenically, it has more in common (as you might expect). Just north of the town of almost sixteen thousand is the stunning, wild scenery of the Parque Nacional de Despeñaperros with its intimidating, stupendous gorges and teeming wild life.

The town's in the province of Jaén, some sixty-six kilometres north of the capital of the same name. If you've got a map of Spain, drop a plumb line from Madrid and it will hang over La Carolina, which is in the middle of countless acres upon countless acres of olive trees that shimmer in the heat (though not today, alas!), marching like a well drilled army over the horizon in every direction, planted in meticulously formal rows, following the constantly changing contours of the earth, creating criss-crossed patterns.

The square was full of little old men, muffled and in flat caps and walking aimlessly up and down the way Spanish little old men do when they've got nothing to do (which seems to be most of the time). Pretending they're busy, they greet each other loudly and like the teenagers they once were half a century and more ago, slap backs and hawk deeply and loudly before spitting accurately, spend an interminable time over a cup of coffee or a glass of red wine, always careful to leave a little in the bottom of the glass.

They drink their coffees with the spoon clamped by a finger inside their cup, which goes a long way to explaining why many Spaniards are either blind in one eye, or have limited view in one or both eyes or walk around with a constant blink.

They're invariably small and squat and heavy-bellied, wear buttoned up shirts without a tie, heavy pullovers, a tooth pick in their mouths, which doesn't stop them talking but threatens at any moment to pierce them in that fleshy place between their nostrils, drawing a trickle of blood and making the eyes water copiously.

Here and there, a grandchild, immaculately dressed and water-combed hair stiff in a quiff, plays in the dust or careers around the square with no direction in mind, making as much noise as is humanly possible, as is the obligatory Spanish way, bless them (most of the time).

Elsewhere, women of all ages come from all directions, laden with shopping, stopping to talk to each other, very possibly about little old men with nothing to do but walk aimlessly up and down, who've had their day and find it hard to accommodate to the present, their past behind them, their futures limited, their male influence (such as it was) largely gone.

I went over to a kiosk in the centre of the square and bought the 'Diario de Jaén' from a black haired, markedly cross-eyed thirty-something, who didn't look too bright. On a whim, I asked him where the Tourist Information Office was. We always like to know where we are, a little of the town's place in the great scheme of things, its reasons for existence, and other things of (relatively) earth shattering importance.

Patiently overlooking my intense stupidity, he wordlessly pointed to the Tourist Information Office – housed in the Town Hall – a few yards away. I felt suitably embarrassed, but tried hard and successfully not to show it, having been in similar positions countless times before in my life. You'd think I'd have learned by now! Sometimes I depress myself, you know.

I went in, passed an open door on my left where two unshaven policemen loitered with no apparent intent, and walked on.

"What do you want?"

I retraced my steps. I literally walked backwards, like an actor in a poor black and white comedy sketch. The attempt at comedy was quite clearly lost on the two policemen, faces like smacked arses.

"Oh, good morning to you, officers. I'm looking for information."

"What sort of information?"

"Tourist information, actually." I tried hard to keep the sarcasm out of my tone, not something I'm very good at, I'm told.

"The office is closed," said the one who bore a striking resemblance to Lee Van Cleef on a very bad day. I decided to kill them with kindness.

"I wonder, perhaps, if you might be able to help. Lovely little place, La Carolina, isn't it! Glad we stopped! Lovely people, and that's the truth! I wonder if you could tell me why La Carolina has a statue of Saint John of The Cross?"

We'd seen a small sign directing us to the statue as soon as we'd driven into the town. It had been a long drive through largely unknown territory from Baeza (where it had absolutely poured down, where 'Saint' Antonio Machado had reluctantly – and unsuccessfully – taught French for what must have seemed more than the seven years he patiently lived there).

The previously sullen face smoothed into what passed for a fulsome smile, and he gently took me by the elbow – the policeman, not Don Antonio, you'll understand. By way of explanation – he clearly had none of any original value, of course, but that wasn't going to deter him – he walked me across the square, chatting companionably, astonished that anyone from Liverpool, England, would stop here in his little town. I don't think he had the slightest inkling where Liverpool was, but that wasn't going to stop him remarking on the matter and presenting himself as an authority on John.

He pointed to a statue ahead and told me that beyond the statue and to the right was the Hermita de San Juan de La Cruz. I thanked him effusively and he saluted me with a flourish, a new found respect, and no small amount of self satisfaction.

We found a white marble statue of the saint, a white column some two metres high behind him, all this on a white marble plinth, the whole surrounded by a tiny garden of flowers, valiant and shivering in the cold sunlight, wrought-iron seats on all four sides.

John, who is the patron saint of La Carolina (along with San Carlos, for some inexplicable reason: why do they want two patron saints?), was actually born miles and miles away in the small Ávila town of Fontiveros in 1542. His real name, as you might guess, was not that by which he is now universally known, but Juan de Yepes Álvarez.

His father died when the boy was very young and his childhood was one of poverty, moving with his mother from place to place in search of work. But he was a bright lad, was John; and after choosing to work in the hospice of Medina del Campo with the absolute down-and-outs, he went to superb Salamanca, where he studied theology and philosophy at the university there.

He then joined the Carmelite Order, and under the tutelage and persuasion of the unique Santa Teresa de Ávila, he joined her single minded crusade to reform the Order. He travelled – walked! – all over Spain, this intensely committed, austere little man, on a mission which would meet no small amount of criticism and even physical opposition from many within the Order.

In 1577, he was even imprisoned in Toledo by fellow Carmelites disaffected (nay, terrified!) by the sweeping changes envisaged by Teresa. Lashed almost on a daily basis, denied the most elementary care and kept in appalling conditions for nine months, he eventually escaped, but not before using his time to write the exceptionally personal poetry for which he is properly famed.

(Let me say here, by way of a related aside, that Stan Hayton and I had to study that same poetry at Liverpool University, top floor of the cavernous Victoria Buildings, in the Truly Wonderful Sixties as part of the

Golden Age Literature course, along with the work of Luis de León. To be honest, we found it taxing in the extreme at times, though even then we could glimpse its worth. But two lads of twenty years of age, hormones – and everything else, for that matter – all over the place, could hardly be expected to empathise with 'The Dark Night of The Soul'! Come on! We did our uttie, as you might expect, and we're now in a better mood to appreciate this exceptional poet – who was also an exceptional saint – whose uncompromising view of the religious life and experience led him to die in southerly Úbeda, just short of fifty years of age.)

So, let's get back to Lee Van Cleef and his directions, the statue of John, and the Hermitage about fifty metres further on.

As Lee indicated, it was on the right hand side. And it was closed. So, what should have been La Carolina's pride and joy – actually, if the truth be told, its only real attraction and claim to fame – was closed to two English Hispanists who would most appreciate the experience of stepping inside. Bugger!

In desultory fashion, we slouched around the tiny building, white and barn-like, with a bulge at one end, atop which was a stone bell tower: impressed and maybe lost by the technicality of the architectural language, aren't you! We made much of trying to open the front door every time a native hove into view, hoping thereby to attract attention to our plight, but with a singular lack of success. San Juan de La Cruz – or 'John', if you prefer – deserved better than this from La Carolina, surely to goodness!

Disappointed in the extreme, cursing colourfully and kicking every little stone with some venom, we wombled back down the slope.

(When I say 'we' in this last statement, it's been pointed out to me that 'we' means 'I'. She would never display disappointment in such an uncivilised, macho manner. I would, though!)

Anyway, coming up the 'paseo' and dressed to the very nines – the

Spanish equivalent is 'made an arm of the sea'! – was a group of about two dozen people, mainly adults. They were on their way to a Baptism: black suits, blindingly white shirts; twenty-something males and their trouser-suited female companions, who would never fall on their faces, so to speak, falling out of halters which signally failed to halt the exaggerated movement of upper-body flesh; the odd granny, sure of her place as the matriarch; the odd grandfather, equally suspecting that his influence was no longer what it might have been in the past, talking tripe in an effort to compensate and roll back the years, nobody listening to him.

All going up to the Church of the Immaculate Conception, which towered over the Hermita. It was a sandstone building with an interesting but unclear architectural style. It looked to be the work of various architects over a considerable period of time with markedly different views about the end product, which at least kept you visually entertained. Part of the church seemed to house a presbytery of unnaturally large proportions, tagged on as an after thought, perhaps.

We briefly thought about asking them about the great mystic, but hastily pushed it from our minds. After all, they were going to a costly Baptism, and in the Spanish way of things they were unlikely to see the inside of a church until the next birth, First Holy Communion, Confirmation, marriage or death.

(It's not like that everywhere, though. In our own tiny church in Tourón, no great distance from Pontevedra, the faithful are indeed very faithful. They sing in full voice, if a little discordantly on occasion, at no fixed point nor for any clearly defined reason at various stages during Mass. It's mildly amusing to hear Galician hymns sung to the tunes of 'Red River Valley', 'The Answer is Blowing in the Wind', and 'The Battle Hymn of The Republic'. It's nothing directly to do with La Carolina, of course, but I thought it would make an interesting comparison and

27

counterpoint. I'm personally waiting for them to compose a Galician hymn to the tune of 'Walk the Line' and I'll out-sing them all!)

We went for a coffee. The man in the coffee shop-cum-bar was a miserable sod and barely registered our presence, serving us with sighs and negligible attention to what he was doing, slopping the coffee in the saucer. So, we drank up, had a wee, paid the bill and left. No tip: Miserable Sod didn't deserve it.

I can't help repeating it: here we are in fame-friendly Andalucía, flamenco and processions, bull fights at five in the afternoon, Federico García Lorca's incomparable poetry, hot sun and undisputed jewels like Granada and Córdoba and Sevilla, black haired men and black eyed women with roses clamped between their teeth (the women, usually), and we're apparently as welcome as a fart at a funeral.

Perhaps they were cold, got out of bed the wrong side, had all had an off-day in La Carolina. Maybe it was us. Whatever the reason, we got in the car, and with no great show of reluctance shook the dust from our feet, driving in silent disappointment generally northwards, up towards eye-wateringly cold Ocaña, and then to Chinchón.

On a more positive note, we quietly recall the kindly young man in the newspaper kiosk (and my hasty, unfounded conclusion as to his level of intelligence: shame on me, yet again! I never learn, do I!), and the briefly excited Lee Van Cleef, and we thanked God for San Juan de La Cruz and other similar mercies.

4. A Orillas del Duero

I have to be honest with you, Reader: four letters into the twenty-seven letters of the Spanish alphabet (the letter 'Ñ' is the extra one), and I'm having a bit of a problem with the letter 'D'. Here's a specimen lot for your consideration.

Derramadero	(meaning 'Overflow' or 'Spillway')
Descargamaría	('Unload Mary')
Dolores	('Pains')
Dos Hermanas	('Two Sisters')

From the very looks of them you'd have to agree with me that they seem, at very least, uninspiring, one or two of them quite clearly dotty. And I'll wager you haven't heard of a single one of them unless – million to one chance, surely – you are reading this chapter and are actually from one of these places. I'd never heard of them before. I looked up the index in the CEPSA Mapamax, increasingly desperate for alternatives.

There is a place we briefly stopped in and know (fairly vaguely) called Daroca, population two thousand plus, which is on the road to Zaragoza, east-north-east of Madrid, no great distance from the quaintly named La Almunia de Doña Godina, a dire place with a spooky feel about it, where we once spent a day and a night in breathless heat, seeing few people (apart from clearly marginalised and unwelcome migrant workers) and speaking to no-one, waiting for the next dawn, when we could leave. But since Margaret can't even remember Daroca, or distinguish it from the hundreds of places we've visited in Spain over more than forty-some years – which is the ultimate insult you could hurl at any town in Spain: she usually remembers them all and has an anecdote for each one, can remember what we ate there! – I think I'll pass that one by.

Another possibility could have been Daimiel. About twenty years or so ago, we were taking Simon down to Úbeda in Andalucía to stay with the listless Bernardo and his very hospitable family. It was August and, after chasing scattered and infrequent clouds in search of momentary shade across Don Quijote's plains of Castilla-La Mancha, we stopped in Daimiel, just short of Almagro, to get out of the suffocating heat. It looked and felt like an abandoned one-horse town from the Old Wild West, and the only thing we were interested in was something ice-berg cold to drink in a bar impervious to heat. Talking rubbish, the result of advanced heat-stroke (and talking rubbish is a gift I have, I'm reliably told by Cael and Mia!), we espied a tiny bar. It was the best bar in all Spain: it had air conditioning.

We drank, one after the other, innumerable glasses of 'Cuarenta y Tres' with Coca Colas to give it a fizz. Simon had endless bottles of 'naranjada'. It was fabulous (but it's the only positive memory we have of Daimiel).

Frankly, I've no appetite to bring either town further to your notice, not that, of themselves, they're not worthy of dalliance and all that. It's just … well, you know. My heart and boundless enthusiasm wouldn't be in it, and you'd soon become aware of the lack of enthusiasm. So, I thought I'd do something different, and tell you about the River Duero. That, as you can see, begins with 'D'.

Machado's River, at almost nine hundred kilometres in length, Spain's third longest river after the Tagus and the Ebro, starts in Duruelo de la Sierra, up in the Picos de Urbión, in the north west of the province of Soria, near the border with Burgos province. It ambles and wombles and splashes westward until it empties in Portuguese Porto, trendy Vila Nova de Gaia on the other bank.

It's called The River of Wine because the surrounding once-arid plains, planted with acres and acres of wheat, produces the more than acceptable Ribera del Duero wines. But for all that, and for the villages and towns and cities it washes or passes through, it's still Machado's River.

Don Antonio was born in southerly Sevilla in 1875, but he'll be forever associated with Castilla and its once empty, sun-baked, windswept countryside of primitive, half-empty villages and its grim, centuries-old poverty. He identified, specifically, with Soria, and with its Duero, whose name is hardly ever absent from his poetry, whether or not directly mentioned. It's there, up in the high hills, as the river 'curves like an archer's bow around Soria', barbican city, where his heart and soul wander.

It's along its banks where this mild mannered man, slightly lugubrious of aspect but with forward-looking, open mind, sought and found in his mid thirties Leonor, the love of his life, less than half his age.

And tragically lost her three years later. To judge from his Duero-inspired poetry, he must have been a lovely, gentle man, not a word said against him. And when he died in 1939, old and tired out beyond his sixty-odd years, in Pyrenean Collioure, fleeing the last days of the merciless Spanish Civil War, he left the Duero engraved in his verse for us.

And the Duero flows on, ever westwards.

Past Almazán, steeped in history, one of the innumerable frontier towns of the Reconquista, the fight to wrest Christian Spain from Moorish domination, whose ownership changed countless times, criss-crossed and shat on by constant conflict; a dozen or more medieval churches and convents and monasteries reflecting the essential role of Christianity and the presence of the Catholic Church over a thousand and more years.

On past Berlanga de Duero, it flows, and its impressive medieval castle, high on a ridge, so the losers could see who was once winning, its population halved in the last forty years as people leave the unforgiving land and head for the cities, tractors and combine harvesters sidelining a diminishing work-force.

Peñaranda de Duero is in Burgos province, its population barely six hundred; castle built, like so many, during the dangerous days of the Reconquista; Main Square, picture-postcard lined with porticoed timber framed buildings; stinking hot under the Castilian summer sun, wincingly cold in winter's wind and snows. And then the Duero gets to Aranda de Duero.

By all contemporary accounts, it was a completely walled town in medieval times, yet another in the long line of bulwarks against the encroaching Moors, finally repelled just before Columbus found the New World (by accident). Now, apart from the Church of Santa María la Real (and a smattering of other monuments of minimal architectural merit), there's little to commend Aranda, surrounded as it is by acre upon sprawling acre of industrial parks, the town a shrine to Michelin, Leche Pascual, and GlaxoSmithKline.

Aranda does have a labyrinth of bodegas running beneath the town centre, storing its precious – and more than pretty good – wines. It also held the BMX World Championship in 2003; has continued to host an important Guitar Festival since 1996; doubled its population to thirty-three thousand since 1970; is twinned with Daira de Yderia in Africa's Western Sahara (Oh, what a coup that was!).

The tedious and ordinary Mariano José de Larra wrote one of his supposedly witty and famous 'artículos' here in 1824 during a short stay; both Galdós and Baroja mention the town in passing in their writing; Miguel Delibes, who's a pretty good writer, visited the town in the 1960s; Hemingway's car, in August 1959, had a puncture here, causing a serious accident from which he walked away unharmed; and some soft bastard backed into John O'Neill's hire-car at a set of traffic lights in the very centre of the town, setting off a colourful volley of non-Spanish oaths that left onlookers open-mouthed and goggle-eyed with its variety and unexpected volume.

So, haste ye forthwith to Aranda de Duero for a good time. God Himself knows what Antonio Cipriano José María Machado Ruiz would make of it. The River Duero, impervious to its surroundings, past and present, simply continues to dawdle westward.

Past Peñafiel, east of Valladolid, with its authentic tenth century Hollywood castle, now the Wine Museum for the whole province of Valladolid, its subterranean bodegas from the fifteenth century. Peñafiel, with its obligatory festivals in memory of the Virgin, and its mock and serious bullfights that go on for a week in mid August in the broiling Castilian sun. But since there must be far more interesting things to do in mid August than to chase and be chased by tons of maddened meat on the hoof; and since I continue to be bemused by the whole event of bullfighting, I, like the stately Duero, will move ever onwards.

Like the river, we'll skirt Valladolid, shall we, where a third of a million people live, surrounded by industry and sprawling industrial parks; where the Catholic Monarchs briefly made their capital, and where poor, penniless, forgotten Christopher Columbus died; where that late-Romantic poet and playwright, José Zorrilla, was born; where young Englishmen came to be trained for the Catholic priesthood prior to their martyrdom in Protestant England; where, somewhat unexpectedly, there are some significant examples of Renaissance art and architecture (and a few nice bars and restaurants, to boot).

Meanwhile, the Duero 'flows and will continue to flow', and no matter how far westward it flows, it's still Antonio Machado's River.

Onwards to Tordesillas, then.

I don't want you to think I'm in any way denigrating Tordesillas and damning it with faint praise when I tell you it's nice. Because that's exactly what it is: nice. In fact, it's very nice indeed in a pleasantly understated way. It seems to have no pretensions about its past and its present, although, of course, it was here that the exceptionally important Treaty was enacted whereby Spain and Portugal carved up between them the newly discovered lands of South America.

The Spanish map-makers, who, one and all, will go down in history as monumental dick-heads of the first order, were so dilatory and inexact in their calculations that the Portuguese, far more aware of the importance of the moment, drew a longitudinal line which gave them the great prize of Brazil, with all its natural resources. Spain was left with countries whose principal geographical features were the awesome, fearsome Andes, the limitless Pampas of Argentina, and the bone-chilling, windswept, inhospitable wastes of Patagonia.

34

We went to the excellent little museum which commemorates the event: copies of original maps and agreements; superb video programmes of quality which bring to light in a clear and attractive manner the whole history of those times; biographies of the principal players. I asked Alan what he thought of it all. He said he was rather impressed by the museum's air-conditioning system.

Thankfully, we two had been to Tordesillas some years before – to its delightfully understated parador, as you might expect – and we'd been impressed by the town's quiet feel of history, its dozen and more significant churches and other religious monuments, all of them worth an extended visit, all redolent with the history of Spain's former greatness. And we liked the utter simplicity and originality of its Main Square, which is everything a Spanish main square should be.

Let me encourage you to retrace your steps a little and stand in front of the Museum of the Treaty of Tordesillas and watch the placid Duero go ambling by no more than one hundred metres in front of you. Down there is where Father John Gerard Feeney and his dog, accompanied as ever by Father Fat Pete, found tasteful accommodation for two nights in August 2010 (and again in August 2011) in a spic-and-span campsite, cooking their steaks, drinking a bottle or two (or three) of goodly Toro red, and contemplating the Duero, the town of Tordesillas, and God, who, once again, was blessing them with His boundless mercies. They watched the sun sink below the horizon as the Duero meandered at their feet in the gathering darkness, on its way to Toro (and beyond, of course).

If you are fortunate enough to have booked a room in Hotel Juan II in Toro, on the side of the building and on the right hand side of the entrance, you'll watch the approach of the Duero from distant, unseen Tordesillas, coming straight towards you over a flat plain which extends on all sides and as far as the eye can see. It then dog-legs at what must be a ninety degree angle, its motion seemingly increased by the rocks and boulders just under the bridge, way below.

"Since Roman times had to be erected a bridge that should unite the Roman camp Villalaz with the City of Toro, the former Arbucala, still, that bridge is not nothing but the forms again repeat in the Romanesque, s.xii century and early xiii, and ashlar occasioned reused. Is very similar to Zamora's Romanesque bridge."

That last paragraph is the English translation offered by an internet site in its description of Toro's sturdy bridge. However, its complete and utter jibberish, with the occasional glimpse of meaning, should not put you off Toro.

We first went there for two reasons: a passing reference (and little more, I have to say) by Laurie Lee in 'As I walked out one midsummer morning', which I first read in one afternoon sitting some forty-plus years ago; and the need to find an overnight stop (with something to commend it) on our four-times-a-year return journeys from Madrid to distant Galicia.

We love Toro unreservedly. We love its simplicity, directness, lack of pretensions, and the fact that in many ways it encapsulates what an authentic Castilian town looks like. We love its bars and its backstreets and its lively Main Square; we love its Colegiata, which we can see from our bedroom window, glorious by day and scintillatingly lit up at night; its summer heat and its bitter cold winter days; its unexplored nooks and crannies, still not completely explored after more than thirty visits, long and short; our walks, on each visit, down the steep incline and across the railway lines to the bridge over the Duero.

We bring friends here and introduce them to Toro and its section of the Duero, which irrigates the huge flatness from horizon to horizon. We sit on the terrace of Hotel Juan II in all weathers and quietly contemplate the dog-legging Duero down below, Tordesillas out of sight to the east,

Zamora equally out of sight, thirty-three kilometres to the west, and there aren't many better experiences in life, I'll tell you. As the sun sinks we go inside and feast on simple Castilian fare and the best of Toro's best wines; take a token walk outside after the meal to see what the stars are doing, to listen to the Duero, far below, still chattering over the rocks and boulders under the bridge.

It reassuringly chatters on, so we contentedly go to bed.

Except for a few bends of little importance, the N122 (sometimes, mystifyingly called the E82) goes on to Zamora (which we'll meet in Chapter 27, if you get that far!), but the river, in anything but a straight trajectory, wiggles and jiggles and turns back on itself times without number, almost playfully, it seems. Passes Zamora wide and deep and flowing more quickly, you sense, as it moves on to its last leg, entering Portugal (where it becomes the Douro) at Salto de Castro. Thereafter, it's anarchic and all over the shop, twisting this way and that over the largely empty countryside, passing the odd inconsequential hamlet of minimal population (even by Portuguese standards), bound for Portuguese Porto, where Birmingham Tony and I got plastered on good Ferreira Ferrinho in the summer of 1965 in one of the 'rabelos' tied up on the river.

> ¡Oh Duero, tu agua corre
> y correrá mientras las nieves blancas
> de enero el sol de mayo
> haga fluir por hoces y barrancas ...
>
> *(Campos de Castilla)*

Quick! Go get yourself a dictionary and try (and try again, and again) to work out the meaning of these wonderfully evocative lines, keep yourself open to the suggestion of the words, and feel fortunate that you've rubbed shoulders with Don Antonio and his river, if only fleetingly.

5. Elorrio 3 - Warrington 0

If we'd lost Tony Lord in Gare d'Austerlitz in the Easter of 1973 (which, at one stage, was a very real possibility) three months before Simon was born, the distinct probability – nay, the certainty! – is that we'd never have got to Elorrio. More important still, we'd have had to go back and explain to twenty sets of justifiably irate Warrington parents why we were once again, but prematurely, in Warrington when we should have been in Elorrio, in the Basque province of Vizcaya. And, oh, by the way, where's Tony Lord, Mr. O'Neill? We can't seem to find him anywhere! We're sure he went with you! And it would not have been easy to explain things, I can tell you.

We'd got the train down to London from Warrington's Bank Key Station, everybody waving and wishing us God-speed (in the local dialect), and then on to Dover without any problem that I can remember. We'd even successfully caught the Calais train to Paris Gare du Nord, shepherding twenty lads through experiences they'd never had before, never even dreamed of having. Don't forget, it's 1973, all but forty years ago, and Warrington kids of that time thought nearby Manchester was almost on the other side of their world.

From Gare du Nord, we three somehow managed to keep together our goggle-eyed charges, moving in generally the right direction, navigating the Paris Métro with only minor difficulty, learning ourselves and making it up as we went along. Getting to Gare d'Austerlitz was, therefore, something of a miraculous achievement in itself. When we eventually located our departure platform to faraway Irún, we were painfully aware that our train was literally within a minute of pulling out, destination the French-Spanish border, twelve long hours away, at very least, and we'd still to haul aboard twenty cumbersome suitcases of various proportions and conditions, some already the worse for wear, onto an already gently moving express, which had not the slightest intention of waiting for a group of twenty-three travellers from Warrington, England.

Happily, we did it: all aboard and bound for glory. Unhappily, some minutes into the journey and presumptuously congratulating ourselves on a job so far well done, and after counting heads, we stopped at nineteen! Nineteen kids! Were there not twenty? Oh, Good Jesus! Can you even start to imagine the panic! Somehow, shouting and tearful, and blaming everything and everyone in existence, we realised who was missing: Tony

Lord, thirteen, tall for his age, willow-slim, blank expression even at the best of times on his sallow, good-natured face. Not a lot going on between his ears, let's say, wouldn't say boo to a goose. But a nice lad, all the same. But not with us!

What to do? Go find a porter, an inspector, a guard, somebody, and use your 1950's grammar-based De La Salle Grammar School (Liverpool) French from Polish Mr. Frankowski's class ('The Vonk') to try to communicate a potential tragedy, as if your face and body language were not already doing a first class job in that department!

Since all the other members of the group had hurriedly scrambled onto the train via the last two carriages – after all, the bastard train was moving, and going faster by the milli-second! – we started our search with the guard's van at the very rear with rapidly vanishing hopes of success and a taste of fear in the mouth. Have you ever felt real, uncomplicated, naked fear? We did.

But, God be forever praised! There, sitting next to the guard, terror on his sallow, good-natured face, eyes bulging and visibly shaking, was Tony Lord from the Sir Thomas Boteler Grammar School, Warrington. On the spot, we swore to mend our ways, light an infinite number of candles to Saint Jude, patron of hopeless cases, say The Rosary every day of our lives. Twice a day. And go to Mass every day, too.

If I were to tell you what happened next it would be at best pure conjecture, but the following can't be all that far from the truth.

Shock, dry mouth, palpitating heart; imprecations of an Anglo Saxon nature which somehow expressed thanks to God Almighty in His Heavens and an enormous earthly relief beyond belief; hugs and tears and recriminations ("You bloody soft little bugger! What happened? Where'd you go, then?"); appallingly ungrammatical thanks to the guard who'd dragged the lad and his suitcase on board a moving express train; a new appreciation of the entire French Nation, God bless every one of them (and let's forget The War altogether, and De Gaulle's visible lack of heartfelt thanks, shall we; and isn't the Marseillaise just about the finest national anthem you've ever heard, isn't it!); cheers and tears as we reunited the lad with the rest of the now deliriously crying but happy group of thirteen year old boys from the Sir Thomas Boteler Grammar School, Warrington.

As to the rest of the journey through the long French night, I can remember nothing, except an overwhelming feeling of relief, though any sleep must have been replete with nightmares and sudden awakenings, hot and cold flushes freely alternating, a churning of bowels and the need for a change of under-crackers, my brother and I up and down the train, checking we hadn't lost anybody else. But I do remember the arrival just after dawn broke in French Hendaye.

Everybody lugging and pushing suitcases across the International Bridge, heaving them onto the train again which carried us at a snail's pace to Irún, no distance to speak of. Trolleys heaped high with suitcases and boxes and livestock; the early morning smell of coffee in the air, and cigars and body odour and chickens and pigs and goodness knows what else. The Smells of Spain. The same smells that had assailed me almost fifteen years earlier on my first, unaccompanied odyssey to meet the wonderful Bartomeu Barceló Roig in Franco's Madrid and then on to Castellón de la Plana via Murcia to stay with the family of Eugenio Gutiérrez López, an architect's friendly but pampered son. The same smells Gerard still remembers from the unforgettable journey of The (equally unforgettable) Class of 1970.

From Irún, we clattered on past San Sebastián in a train that might have been a luxurious way to travel in the nineteenth century. But in 1973, it's all hard, wooden, upright seats, overhead luggage racks full of livestock, Basque peasants in their Basque berets, unshaven faces and pungent cigars – the menfolk, too! – and most of our party hanging on perilously to overhead straps, tired beyond sleep, but somehow proud of our limited achievement so far: we were fast bonding. And this train goes to Durango, lads.

This is the same railway junction town with its small arms factories that was dive-bombed and machine-gunned by Hitler's Condor Legion on 31 March, 1937, almost eight months after the outbreak of the horrendous Spanish Civil War (of despicable memory). One hundred and twenty-seven people were killed on that day in Durango. A further one hundred and twenty-one later died in the town's hospitals as a result of their injuries. Four weeks later, on 28 April – Guernica having been systematically destroyed two days previously, that destruction blamed on the Basques themselves, would you believe it – Durango fell without resistance. You need to know these things from the comfortable remove of the twenty-first century, don't you agree. Rhetorical question. No punctuation marks needed. And these are undeniable, human facts, and tragedies, not just a list of figures. Not just the 'Special Subject' I did with Derek Lomax at Liverpool University in 1965, all facts and academic study.

I suppose – I can't possibly remember with any sort of accuracy – that we waited around in Durango's rebuilt railway station for an equally decrepit train; hauled our luggage aboard; fell asleep standing or sitting or hanging from another set of straps above our heads; eventually arrived in Elorrio, jiggered beyond description, all twenty-three of us, glad to be stationary for the first time in thirty-six action packed hours.

My brother (for almost twenty years) and I (for two relatively unhappy years) taught at the Sir Thomas Boteler Grammar School, and were committed to coaching lads in football at a time when watching professional football was still both affordable and entertaining (unlike nowadays, when complete dick-heads and other nonentities are paid astronomically high wages for the production of minimal ability, animal behaviour, and unsociable, antisocial traits. Do you remember, as a counterpoint, 'Shirley' Temple's explosive winner for Everton in the 1968 Cup Final, and his almost embarrassed return to the centre circle to be congratulated by his colleagues in gentlemanly fashion? Fast forward to today's 'sporting' specimens and their childlike, embarrassing antics.)

In spite of being in Rugby League Land, many of the kids relished the opportunity to play football, and we two, amongst others, loved coaching them.

To cut a long story short, my brother had decided to take a group of thirteen year old lads to play a few matches in the Basque Country. Why he'd chosen Elorrio I can neither remember nor guess at, though in all probability it was the only reply he received to the many letters he'd sent. My roles were to run the financial side of the venture – to dole out the pocket money and pay the bills, in essence, though 'financial side' sounds a bit better – act as second (and very secondary) coach, and, not least, to be the number one fanatical cheer leader.

A gentle man – and a gentleman – called Jim Ryan, quietly spoken history teacher and confirmed bachelor, would also come along to improve the ratio of teachers-to-children. The fact that he could, and did, with alarming ease, fall asleep in any situation and at any hour at the drop of a hat meant that the ratio was not quite as good as it seemed at first sight. Jim could never stay awake on any means of transport, moving or otherwise, for which he frequently and profusely apologised: fast asleep before the coach was in first gear, and that after breakfast, too. And a good night's sleep, too. Snoring, but gently.

We stayed in the boarding section of the secondary school on the edge of Elorrio run by a religious order of Catholic priests. Distant recall remembers it as a gaunt structure, built like the proverbial brick shit-house in the Basque manner, presumably to keep out the cold and the mountain mists. Accommodation was in a dormitory which ran the length of the front of the school, with the result that nights were frequently musical, punctuated with all manner of snores and grunts and farts of various intensity, with nightmares and belches, to say nothing of the sleepwalkers. But we all loved every minute of it. It was simply a fabulous experience.

We were fed wholesome, sturdy meals of mountainous proportions, in the Basque manner. And even sturdier alcoholic drinks. Jim loved the food (and the drinks, the home brewed 'licores', to which there seemed to be no limit, either in quantity or variety, and it made for pleasant evenings, in spite of the cold. Jim said it helped him sleep after a busy day of football training and coaching and bracing mountain air and trying to stay awake).

I think we played three competitive games in all against local sides. In anticipation of the trip, we'd told them by letter the age range of our twenty kids, with the request that the priests should arrange games against Spanish teams of similar (hopefully identical) age and pedigree. But each team we played seemed bent on a war of attrition and revenge for the Armada, fielding lads who had quite obviously started shaving years previously, and who were, on average, a metre taller than the Warrington lads. They kicked the very shit out of our lads, and bare-facedly included 'ringers' in every one of the three games we played, which somehow nullified the 'friendly' nature of the sporting encounters. I rather think our lads lost all three games, though they gave spirited performances, especially when they successfully kicked back in retaliation, having realised that the priest-referee was half blind, at best, and didn't seem to have any remote idea of the rules.

It wasn't all football, of course. We hired a coach to explore the coast and the interior: picturesque harbour towns like Zumaia and Bermeo and Leikeitio, Zarautz and Ondárroa; Mundaka, where Pat Seeley spent every summer with 'her' Basque family; Amorebieta and Zumárraga; Azkoitia and Azpeitia; Durango, though I can't remember why, given its past history and 1973 drabness; and we even spent a wonderful day in San Sebastián, eating prodigiously well. I do recall very vividly having to wake up the coach driver on the numerous occasions he slumped over the steering wheel on the bends as well as the straights. This being the Basque Country, there were bends aplenty.

My brother and I took the kids hiking in the hills on a few occasions, joining in the snowball fights, which often drew blood, all against the background of snow-clad, towering peaks and rolling hills, to the sounds of cow bells and what we were later told was ETA rifle fire in the unseen distance.

Of the town of Elorrio, at this remove of almost forty years, I have little more than an indistinct memory, but I do recall substantial houses and 'palacios' (what we'd call, perhaps, minor stately homes or mansions), with their sombre facades relieved by enormous stone coats of arms. It's when you travel elsewhere in Spain, you realise just how different in most ways the Basque Country is from places like enchanting Extremadura, Andalucía (most certainly), and even nearby Asturias and Cantabria (with their own mountains and pastures).

And the people, too, are different in ways it's not always easy to pinpoint, both physically and otherwise. Short, sturdy people, with what you might euphemistically call faces of 'character', rather than handsome; faces you hope 'they'll grow into', sturdy in every sense of the word, with their insistence that they aren't Spaniards, much to the annoyance or disdain of the rest of Spain. Independent people, forcefully so, with their own history and culture and, most especially, their language, which has not the remotest association with Castilian Spanish, nor any other European language, if it comes to that. Ask a Castilian, for example, what that street name over there means and he'll immediately tell you he hasn't got a clue. Here's an example: the Castilian Spanish word for 'headmaster' is 'director', which, I dare to say, would be understood by everyone. The Basque equivalent is 'zuzendari'. Point taken, I presume.

Respectful people, that's for sure, though certainly formal and distant with us back in 1973. Perhaps they'd had less than complimentary reports about Warrington lads. Perhaps they didn't like Rugby League. But the inhabitants of Elorrio visibly (and, regrettably) failed to warm in any significant way to the novel presence in their midst of twenty friendly kids and their three teachers (two of whom, closely related, were dynamic and committed, shall we say, and open to social intercourse). There was by no means anything unpleasant about them, nothing you could put your finger on, but not at all open and friendly like other people we'd mixed with in similar circumstances the length and breadth of Spain. Sadly, after our adventure, we never had any reply to our further correspondence. I don't know what conclusions you want to draw about that.

Of course, the 'troubles' and ETA and the Basque feeling of alienation from the rest of Spain – which a significant number of Basques seem happy to perpetuate, it must be said – might have had something to do with that. And, of course, that was almost forty years ago and the natural reserve of the Basques might just have changed a tad in that time (though not their political persuasions). And the entire population of Elorrio might well have got out of the wrong side of bed for the whole week or so we were there. That's another possibility.

And the thought occurs to me that in these twenty-first century days of teachers having to account for their every action and word, such an adventure would no longer be possible. That's a shame, it really is. There's only one loser there.

6. Frómista

Right, now! Hands up anybody who's been to Frómista! Nobody? Honestly? Well, let's do it another way, shall we? Hands up anybody who knows where Frómista is, then! No? Well, erm … Anybody know anything about Frómista? Anybody ever heard of Frómista? Honestly? Sure? OK, then, let's start again, only differently, shall we, and see where we go from there. Agreed? Agreed!

Well, now, once upon a time – actually it was in the year 711 AD – a gang of well trained, completely ruthless, unbelievably ambitious, fanatically dedicated Berbers (mostly Arabs) from North Africa, swarmed across what's now called the Straits of Gibraltar, and within seven – seven! – short years they'd subdued the entire Peninsula (except for the extreme north west, of course, though they did make some inroads). Their task, such as it was, was helped in no small measure by the fractious nature of the existing Christian kingdoms of Spain, scattered hither and thither, with their squabbling monarchs (frequently bastards, in both senses of the word) and nobles, invariably at each others' throats.

But the Moors – we'll call them that to simplify matters – were then very briefly held up in the northerly mountains of Covadonga by just thirty Christian warriors who, in 718, slaughtered no fewer than 124,000 of the enemy (not a misprint, by the way!). Spaniards love legends and hyperbole and you can't get much more hyperbolic than that, now, can you! Feel free to pause here to reconsider these figures.

There followed, for the next (almost) eight hundred years, what is generally referred to as La Reconquista. What it was supposed to be was the Christian attempt to rid Spain of the Moors, eject Islam, and re-establish Christianity. What it turned out to be was something significantly different, in no small way due to the fact that Christian kings and princes and nobles didn't trust each other long enough to establish anything remotely similar to a common cause.

Happily for the Christians, internal Moorish dissent and disputes meant that Moorish rule was sometimes a little fragmented, with the result that Christians eventually learned to live side by side with the invaders. Except for the odd series of blood-lettings, Moor and Christian were remarkably tolerant of each other, given the circumstances, though there was never any doubt who was top dog.

One such top dog was al-Mansur who, judging the Christians to be in need of reminding who ruled whom, struck the fear of God (or Allah) into them. He even briefly got as far as Galician Santiago de Compostela and swiped the bells from the bell tower of the recently built, standard-bearer cathedral. To add insult to injury, he had these same iconic bells transported to southern Córdoba, almost one thousand kilometres distant. Hell of an undertaking just to make a point, you'd think.

("Hang on a second! All very interesting, but what's this got to do with … what's it called? … this place, Frómista, then? I thought we were talking about that. I don't get the connection. Perhaps …"

"Patience, and all will be revealed in the sweet by and by.")

Whilst Moor and Christian were (relatively) seldom at each others' throats on a regular basis, it began to dawn on those Christian kingdoms of Spain that still maintained a small measure of independence that they needed a unifying force. They needed a standard bearer. Or a flag. Or something. Something to get them all singing from the same hymn sheet, even if slightly out of tune.

By happy chance, along came a Galician shepherd, a loaf and a wedge of 'tetilla' in one hand, a flagon of 'orujo' in the other, slightly tipsy, a satisfied but vacant look on his weathered face, little between his ears, shall we say, reporting that he'd seen this bright star shining down on a particular field. Nothing new in that, you might feel: stars tend to shine by nature, and can frequently be seen from below.

On examination, lo and behold, but didn't they discover the very place where the Apostle James was buried! Quick as a flash, up went a grand church to celebrate the find, the ninth century basilica erected by King Alfonso II being the site where the present eleventh-to-thirteenth century cathedral now majestically stands. Praise the lord and pass the 'orujo'. And the 'tetilla'!

James had been what we'd probably call a missionary in Spain after the death of Jesus. Eventually, as you might have expected of those times, he was beheaded by the Romans for upsetting the status quo, but his nearest and dearest had managed to row his body from Rome to what is now somewhere in the region of Finisterre. If you get a chance, look up a simplified map of present day Europe and marvel at their achievement. In a rowing boat, too! Well, I'll go to the foot of our stairs, as my Mother would have said.

So, the cult of Saint James Matamoros (Killer of Moors) was born and started to flourish. Single-handedly, he and his white horse – white for 'the goodies', don't you know – led the Christians to victory over the Moors at the Battle of Clavijo in 846. The fact that there's absolutely no historical proof of the authenticity of the battle ever having taken place mattered not a jot. It boosted the morale of Christian Spain and the importance of Santiago de Compostela (it means 'field of stars') as a hallowed place of pilgrimage, a viable alternative to Rome and Jerusalem.

("But what about this Frómista, then? What's all this Moors and Christians and stars and shepherd with 'tetilla' and 'orujo' got to do with it, eh?"

"Nearly there! Hold hard!")

Nowadays, it's generally thought that the Road to Santiago de Compostela – the so called French Road, because most pilgrims came via south-west France and onwards thereafter – starts 'properly' near St-Jean-Pied-de Port, thence to Basque Puente de la Reina, through Logroño to Burgos to León to Santiago. And, as far as generalisations go, that's probably acceptable – except, of course, for the fact that truthful history is never quite as simple as that, nor does 'popular' history tell all the facts. And, for your information, there's at least eight – yes, eight! – different Roads to Santiago.

("And Frómista? Are we getting any closer?")

To simplify matters, let's say you've got as far as Castilian Burgos, El Cid's city, all traffic and a fine Gothic cathedral, and you're still just under six hundred kilometres east of your destination. On you go westward, ever westward, Pilgrim, through hamlets like Hornillos del Camino to Castrojeriz to Itero del Castillo to Boadilla del Camino, and here we are, at last, in Frómista (thank God and Saint James!).

("You can say that again!")

Goodness knows what the population of Frómista was in medieval times, but there are only eight hundred or so inhabitants now, half its population in 1960. And it's true to say that its fame, such as it is, is of the past, though it's the past that supports the present in the shape of the exceptionally beautiful little Church of San Martín de Tours (born in Hungary, you might like to know).

("So what's he doing here, then?"

"Hush up and stop asking awkward questions! Anyway, I don't know.")

Centrally placed along the Camino Francés, the first officially documented mention of the church was in 1066 (of all things!) when the first stone was laid. By the mid thirteenth century, it was completed and functional, though this happy state was not to last any great time: Spain was replete with churches and religious monuments of one sort or another, and their upkeep could be pretty expensive, too. From the fifteenth century, it entered a steady period of decline and was eventually abandoned completely and closed down as unfit for use. There's a dining-table-sized model near the altar of the church showing its architecturally worst state, which makes you appreciate what happened thereafter.

Then, along comes Aníbal Álvarez y Amoroso, God bless him, an architect of vision and singular dedication, no doubt, who undertook the complete renovation of the church in 1894. Ten years later, it was indeed completed. It's Romanesque in design and is generally accepted as being the most perfect example of its class in all Spain (which is saying a lot, since the Province of Palencia alone has dozens of Romanesque churches which are blindingly beautiful. Oh, and did you know – I didn't until comparatively recently – that the first university in Spain, dating from 1208, is in the humble, tourist-shy city of Palencia? Now there's a thing! Tell your friends.).

We always insist that the bus driver take Pax Travel Pilgrims to see the Church of San Martín, tiny Frómista's only real historical claim to fame; and invariably they are in awe and admiration of it, recognising its unique design and the pivotal role it plays in the cult of Saint James, the sheer simplicity of its beauty and its perfect proportions. Mind you, some of them would slope off to the first bar or café as soon as we dock, given half a chance, unless and until they're prevailed upon to "Just come and see this church first: you'll kick yourself if you miss it".

We were once sitting on the low wall that surrounds the church, waiting for opening time (and the free guided tour) and got talking to an English lady – forty or so, I suppose – and her twelve year old son. They were pilgrims walking to Santiago. They were decidedly taciturn, but not unfriendly, and we talked 'around' their pilgrimage, rather than 'head on'. They looked tired, somewhat preoccupied, but quietly resolved to go on. They'd spent the night in the pilgrims' 'albergue' around the back of the church, fewer than one hundred metres away.

They didn't say exactly why they had come. Everyone, it seems, has a different reason (which, realistically, can hardly have changed very much during the twelve-hundred year history of the Camino). Walking – in the main – or by bicycle – less frequently – some come for the sheer adventure and test of will that The Road presents; others, to slow things down and take a good look at themselves, where they are in their lives, spiritually or otherwise; whilst others – who knows what percentage? – come for a specifically religious reason. And they come from just about every country.

Of course, as you might expect, there's always a greater number in Holy Year, which is when the feast of Saint James, Spain's patron saint, 25 July, falls on a Sunday. The year 2010 was such an occasion: the next one will be 2021. The good and the not so good and the politicians came and were much in evidence, most especially, and almost exclusively, at journey's end, the Cathedral of Santiago de Compostela. The King and Queen came, and Pope Benedict, all the way from Rome, and a host of other worthies. But not that little shit, José Luis Rodríguez Zapatero, leader of the PSOE (Spain's ruling Socialist Party in this year of 2011) and President of Spain. He not so tacitly refused to turn up.

Of course, nobody's suggesting for one moment that Zapatero has any obligation to go to Santiago. On an official level, as head of the Spanish government, he arguably should have gone, if only to represent his government and the Spanish people in a place which is of singular significance in the history, culture and legacy of Spain (just as 'Muslim' Córdoba and Granada surely are) and, especially, in a Holy Year in the presence of another Head of State (the Vatican State, in this instance). But he didn't: not once. It wasn't that he didn't have the time or the opportunity: this very small minded, haunted-looking public servant wanted to make an embittered point and exhibit his openly anti-clerical stance (to say nothing of his appalling bad manners).

ABC reported him as saying the following (which he doesn't deny): "What do they want, then? For us to follow a policy laid down by the Pope? It's us who will make laws that the citizens of our country want" (which, by the way, is not being questioned); and then, directly aimed at the Catholic Church in Spain, he said: "For decades and decades they have forced us to accept the codes of conduct of a specific way of viewing life and religion. The great majority of our people want to be free, unwilling to have their morality imposed on them". (Nor your jaundiced views, pillock!)

Jesus! Does this myopic nonentity have nothing more pressing on his agenda at the moment? The continued problems in the Basque Provinces or the dire state of the economy, for example? The debilitating effects of rising unemployment, most especially of those under thirty years of age, presently running at 45%? The abuse of political power and the existence of open, visible fraud in high places wherever you look? The internal political strife in his own party, many of whom are ready to stab him in the back at the earliest opportunity? Maybe he's afraid of the Basques. Maybe he hasn't got a clue on the economy (which is a view shared by an alarming number of Spaniards, to judge from the frequent polls carried out by newspapers of all political persuasions, damning him for his inactivity. He tends to smile, when confronted by criticism, in an inane fashion, which makes you wonder if he's all there).

With just a bit of luck, this failed public servant (that's what he is, you know, a public servant, whichever way he looks at it) will have cut his own political throat, because, in spite of the general lukewarm attitude towards religion and the Spanish Church and the Sacraments, in spite of the latent anti-clericalism which is so much a part of the Spanish psyche, a significant percentage of Spaniards still consider themselves Catholics (though not as we English interpret it, I hasten to add!). They may not go to Mass on Sunday but they'll still tell you they're Catholics, still want Baptisms and marriages and funerals performed in a Catholic church.

Thankfully, his shameful outburst in Vilacans in late 2010 will have minimal (if any) effect on the cult of Saint James, the Road to Santiago, or the inhabitants of sleepy Frómista (always assuming they know who Zapatero is, which is extremely doubtful). And we and Pax Travel Pilgrims and thousands more will continue to sit in front of the Church of San

Martín de Tours and take pleasure in our shared friendship and adventures on the Camino Francés, and this absolutely stunning monument to the continued belief of a very significant number of pilgrims. And Frómista will continue to welcome its pilgrims.

So, cop for that, Zapatero!

7. Garabandal

It's surely got to be 'G for Granada', hasn't it, the place of dreams, according to Segovia, where the Lord 'put the seed of music into my soul'.

This is the city which became the focal point for the Moors, who spent almost eight hundred years in Spain, arriving in 711 as a motley but highly disciplined band of invaders, bent on subjugating the whole of the Iberian Peninsula to their will. This is the city which, from 1238 until 1492, witnessed its own Golden Age of gifted artisans and merchants and scholars and scientists of every discipline, investing Granada with an international reputation as an important centre for learning and culture; thereafter, to be followed by the Renaissance splendour initiated and encouraged by the Reyes Católicos, Fernando and Isabel. This is the city of the fantastic Alhambra Palace and the imposing Generalife, with its gardens of 'lofty paradise'.

Along with Sevilla (and possibly with Córdoba joining that elite of the Andalusian Trinity), Granada, redolent with history on the grandest of scales, is symbolic of Spain and all things Spanish, perhaps more than any other city in Spain. Even on an utterly popular level – and leaving aside the relative aberrations that are Torremolinos and Nerja and even big, unwieldy Málaga – you say 'Spain' and up pops Granada nine times out of ten.

Yet, in spite of all that, and for the purposes of this book, it won't be 'G for Granada' (sorry!) for the simple reason that – shame on me! – I don't know Granada well enough to be able to record memories or opinions of any significant or reliable value.

The one and only time we went there, in the summer of 1988, was after we'd dropped off Simon in oven-hot Úbeda. On the way northwards, in search of less heat and familiar surroundings (and more hospitable surroundings, I might add), we spent a restless, unmemorable night in a fairly nondescript hotel in Granada – Margaret can't even remember the name or the approximate location, so that should tell you something! – with every intention of going up to the Alhambra the next day. Getting there shortly after an early breakfast, we discovered a queue in excess of some two hundred metres already formed in twenty-eight degrees of heat. We were prepared to put up with this in the interests of culture-hunting, but we were assailed at every turn by shady, swarthy characters aggressively 'offering' their totally unofficial and unnecessary services as to where we could park the hire-car, demanding money up-front for the questionable privilege, a malicious glint in their eyes if we refused. Not for the first time in our travels, we were less than happy in Andalucía, invariably feeling slightly out of place. Perhaps that's our fault: I freely confess that we've never warmed to it in the same way as we have with northern Spain.

We high-tailed it out with scarcely a backward glance, bound for cooler climes well north of Madrid, where we have always been more culturally-comfortable, where Catherine was waiting impatiently to be picked up after a week of semi-starvation with Angelina and her new-age family on Cantabria's coast.

John Ronnie Holdsworth's Gijón was another possibility, in so far as it begins with the letter 'G'. But this big city of 270,000, the largest in the Principality of (beautiful) Asturias, and little more than an industrial port, largely rebuilt after the cruel bombardments of the equally cruel Spanish Civil War, has relatively little to commend it, however hard the Tourist Board tries to convince you otherwise. Sorry, Ronnie, we have tried!

Neither does Guadalajara nor Girona inspire enthusiasm to any remotely significant extent. So it has to be Garabandal. Or, to give it its full name, San Sebastián de Garabandal.

"Where is it?"

"Beg pardon?" I say, slightly taken off guard by the unexpected question from Spaniards who, you might expect, should know their own geography.

"Where is it? Where's this Garabandal place?"

"You don't know? You're the Spaniard, not me."

And that's, more or less, what every Spaniard without exception says to me when I mention in conversation that we spent five days in late September, 2011, with twenty-eight elderly Australians – Australians, of all people! – in a tiny village of under one hundred people, one road in, the same road out, in the middle of the middle of nowhere, somewhat incongruously bestowed with three guest-houses, praying to Our Lady, singing hymns, attending two Masses a day, climbing rutted paths and steep hills whilst saying countless Rosaries, and eating the finest food we've ever eaten in Spain, or anywhere else, come to that, for many years.

When Pax's London office asked us to do the guiding – starting in Lisbon, where we temporarily but worryingly lost one pilgrim, on to Portuguese Fátima, to Santiago de Compostela, where Margaret spent three long hours in hospital with the party's spiritual leader, the final destination being Paris via Lourdes via TGV – we asked them for a few minutes grace before making our decision: we'd never in our lives heard of Garabandal, so out came CEPSA's trusty Mapamax 2009.

Straight to the index at the back we went, because we hadn't the faintest notion where it might be, even by means of guesswork or a process of elimination or drawing on our immense experience over fifty years getting wonderfully, joyfully lost in Spain's varied geography.

"It's on page five, co-ordinates D3."

"And?"

"Well, leave Ribadesella up there on the north coast and keep going east. Pass Llanes, and when you get to Unquera, find the CA 181. It's a bugger of a track that wiggles this way and that. Then you get to a place called Puentenansa. You can't miss it. Well, you can if you're not watching, because it's nothing more than a knot of rural-looking houses (as you might expect, being in the middle of a rural nowhere) with smoking chimneys and little sign of life. A bit further on, there's a sign for Cosío, which you'll miss if you blink – the village, I mean, not necessarily the sign, though probably both – and then keep a look-out for another sign saying San Sebastián de Garabandal.

"Oh, thanks. Clear as mud. Must go there for a good time. What, pray tell, were you two doing there, then?"

So, we told them about the twenty-eight elderly Australians and the fact that they'd come half way around the world from Brisbane and Melbourne via Dubai and Madrid and Lisbon; that the priest had a horrendous accident in the cathedral of Santiago de Compostela – his own fault, I might add, and he would agree – after which he became the most sociable person you could imagine (well, almost), a veritable miracle; that the pilgrim who went astray in Lisbon airport managed to do the same two weeks later in Charles de Gaulle airport until we tied him to his luggage trolley; that they quite liked Oviedo and managed to beat even Spaniards to front seats in the cathedral, refusing to budge when asked; that we prayed a lot and sang a lot and processed up steep hills and watched a lot of videos about Garabandal before going to bed, Billy Velasco (for once not quoting John, 23) snoring raucously as soon as the lights went out, much to his wife's embarrassment; that Ronnie, the Indian-Australian train-driver and country-music fan of George Jones and Johnny Cash and Alison Kraus and The Cox Family, bought a life-size statue of Our Lady of Fatima and lugged it all over Portugal, Spain and France, leaving the other two hefty cases for his wife to carry, intending somehow to get it (and his wife, presumably) back to Melbourne; that we spent five days in a remote village where the child population is precisely three and old-age is the norm.

It wasn't always like this, of course. Fifty years ago, four young girls – Conchita González, Mari Luz González, Jacinta González (none of them related) and Mari Loli Monzón – got the shock of their twelve year old lives. They were playing, as the kids of the village did, up in the hills just above their houses, and Saint Michael the Archangel appeared to them. He came with a flash and a boom and then he was gone: that's how they described it. It was Sunday evening, 18 June, 1961, and the event was to change their little lives and, to a certain extent, the life of the village of San Sebastián de Garabandal (though not as much as you might expect).

It was actually called San Sebastián by the inhabitants, then plain Garabandal, then finally San Sebastián de Garabandal, so as not to be confused with San Sebastián in the Basque province of Guipúzcoa. Why such a differentiation was thought necessary is way beyond me, since San Sebastián de Garabandal is in Cantabria; and, more to the point, surely nobody would confuse mountain-bound San Sebastián de Garabandal, with its hundred-odd inhabitants, with the coastal city of San Sebastián and its 180,000 inhabitants, light years ahead in every conceivable respect.

Anyway, back to Saint Michael. He was there to tell the girls that within a couple of weeks Our Lady herself would appear to them; and on the very first day of July, she appeared for the first time. Naturally, they ran home half terrified to tell their mums and dads and anybody else within listening distance (which was the entire village, given its size). So, when Our Lady appeared the next day, everyone was camped around and in between the nine pine trees that overlooked the village (and still do). Priests and local dignitaries and people of worth and people of questionable worth from outlying villages came too, to see for themselves.

Over the next four years, Our Lady appeared to the children on more than two thousand occasions – yes, two thousand – and each time the girls went into a deep trance. They failed to react to pins plunged into their bodies, burning matches held against their skin, bright lights shone directly into their eyes, crashing falls against the rocks beneath their feet. Grown men could not lift them off their feet, and, in their headlong dash down the mountain (sometimes backwards), they outpaced everyone. On all occasions, they levitated. We two, and the Australians, actually spoke to some of the villagers, and they were adamant that such things happened. They saw them: simple as that, and no room for a shadow of doubt.

As you might expect, there were those who did doubt the whole thing, so that when the news quickly leaked out beyond the village, and beyond the few surrounding villages, priests and psychiatrists and doctors and men of learning and renown flooded into the little village. Most, of course, were more than a little suspicious about the whole thing. Whilst this sort of thing wasn't exactly a daily event in Christendom, isn't it strange that it's the backward, isolated places that always lay claim to such extraordinary events! Think of Lourdes and Fátima and Medjugorje for starters.

One of the original doubters was Father Luis Andreu, a Jesuit theology professor and a man of considerable academic clout. His first reaction was of utter incredulity. By the end of the first week in August, five weeks after the continuing apparitions of Our Lady, he changed his mind completely and became an unshakeable believer. In the early hours of the morning following his change of mind, whilst being driven away from Garabandal, he died peacefully in the car. Make of that what you will.

Two months later, Our Lady told the four girls that only prayer, penance and sacrifice could save mankind – shades of the children of Fátima and Bernadette Soubirous and Lourdes.

After January 1963, whilst the rest of the Catholic world carried on with their lives in almost total ignorance of Garabandal and the appearances, the apparitions ceased, except for Conchita; and up at the pines, Our Lady gave her the direst warnings yet: that 'many cardinals, many bishops, many priests are on the road to perdition, and are taking many souls with them'; that this was the final warning. The last appearance was in November of that same year.

Let's pause. Go back and read all that again. Transport yourself, if you can, to a back-of-beyond peasant village of a dozen or so houses whose contact with the outside world was minimal in the extreme, probably limited to nearby Cosío (it still is!). Try to imagine what you'd feel. Jesus, you'd think to yourself, why here, of all places! And it must have put the very fear of God right up the archbishops and bishops and priests whom Our Lady was unequivocally criticising in the clearest terms!

And so, you'll ask yourself, how did the Catholic Establishment and Rome react to all this?

That's the funny thing (as in 'funny-peculiar') about it, because although the Catholic Church – or 'Rome', if you'd prefer – doesn't seem to have taken its usual conservative line with what at first sight appears to be something bordering on the miraculous, neither has it condemned it. It's as if things have been left in abeyance, and nobody knows what to do next.

According to the National Garabandal Centre, which is based in Queensland, Australia – er, why not Madrid, Spain, or Rome, Italy? – the events of Garabandal are under investigation, with no final judgement yet made. It seems like a cop-out to me, personally. 'Leave it alone and it might go away,' you can almost hear them say.

And considering that it's fifty years since the apparitions started, it's amazing (to us two, at least) that nobody but zealots and those obsessed with Garabandal (and Australians. Australians!) seem to show the remotest interest in these events that are so totally inadequately publicised in Spain.

"I've never even heard of the place."

"Exactly my point, little Spanish buddy," I reply.

I do know from my own direct contact with him that the parish priest, Father Rolando, a man of immense elegance and sincerity, doesn't want to turn it into another Fátima (and so say all of us to that one!). And I do know twenty-eight elderly and sincere and down-to-earth Australians who are determined that the facts and message of Garabandal will become more widely known. And therein resides the problem.

Perhaps what most impresses us about Garabandal (whether we're sympathetic to it or not) is that it's most un-Spanish: it's not noisy nor spectacular nor exhibitionist. We two have travelled the length and breadth of Spain, and have been suitably impressed (to one extent or another), with the Spaniards' 'celebration' of religion and religious events. We've seen Santiago de Compostela, of course, on numerous occasions, with its throngs of noisy pilgrims and visitors, walking and chatting companionably and taking photographs whilst the Mass has been celebrated; witnessed their gratuitous noise in the monastery of Guadalupe until a priest told them in no uncertain terms to 'Shut up and listen to me whilst I'm talking, and don't forget you're in the House of God'; seen the herds in the Cathedral of León, snapping photos and strolling and talking aloud; watched the invited dignitaries in the Cathedral of Oviedo on their once-a-year incursion into a religious building, completely lost as to what is expected of them, when to stand, when to sit; witnessed countless Holy Week processions, some of which, frankly, were an excuse for a dress-up and a piss-up; watched well-intentioned catechists preparing kids for the Sacraments in our own little Galician church, more interested in the manner of making the Sign of the Cross correctly (and in exhibitionist fashion) than in getting the kids interested in what really happens in church, what it's really all about, to the extent that they might keep attending after First Communion and Confirmation.

But Garabandal's somehow different. It's quiet and remote (in every sense) and aware of its unique experience; its elderly inhabitants see their church, presently being refurbished, as a central feature in their daily lives; and there's not the slightest indication that they intend, in any way, to exploit things: quite the opposite. They're hostile to any intrusions (and there have been a few, let me tell you). In its way, it's impressive in its honesty and sincerity.

Meanwhile, this tiny village, with its three modest guest houses and two tiny (religious) gift shops and one inconspicuous bar, continues to exist; and that's the feeling you distinctly get, that it's 'existing', waiting for whatever comes next, without any clear idea in mind as to what the future will be. A limbo existence that's been going on for fifty years, and that doesn't appear to be about to change any day soon.

And we two came away perplexed by it all, uncertain about our own feelings. And that's not like us, I have to tell you.

8. Costa del Vino

For no other reason than the fact that we didn't know it as well as other parts of Spain, we decided to go to La Rioja prior to continuing on to our ultimate destination of Reinosa, deep in the south of verdant Cantabria, to see Chuchi and The Girls. We'd walk, and talk about old times, and dine with them, and enjoy their company, tell and re-tell stories about kids from Saint Mary's we'd taken there over twenty-five years until they bore a passing resemblance to the absolute truth. Although Logroño is indisputably the capital of La Rioja by dint of its size (one hundred and forty thousand souls) and its role as the commercial centre of the region, we decided to look elsewhere and leave Logroño for, perhaps, another time.

I can't explain to you – simply because I now no longer know or recall – why we'd come up via Guadalajara and Calatayud, though careful not to stop off in either place, given experiences we'd prefer not to share, if that's all the same to you. We did stop the night in a God-foresaken, one-horse, back-of-beyond little town called La Almunia de Doña Godina, and moved off at first light after an entire night of summer thunder and lightning to a place called Tarazona, west of mighty Zaragoza and just about inside the borders of otherwise captivating Aragón. We got there in mid afternoon.

In spite of the fact that it was mid-August, it rained so hard and so unexpectedly (and so unexpectedly hard) when we were literally getting out of the car, that within the hour the lowly waters of the River Quieles rose alarmingly, sending torrents of chocolate-coloured mud down all the streets leading into the main square. The rain stopped around seven o'clock: I remember the time, because that's when we finally managed to arrive at the doors of the Tourist Information Office (and my contretemps with the foolish teenaged girl they were then employing there).

Prior to this, we'd never heard of the River Quieles, but we remembered it thereafter and frowned. Not even in Kuala Lumpur's rainy season had we seen such amounts of water. On we went to Calahora for our first experience of La Rioja.

It's quite a big place by local standards, with twenty thousand inhabitants. On a huge, nicely flower-stocked roundabout in the centre of town, there's an important sign, presumably for visitors, informing you that Calahora offers – and I quote, having incredulously made a written note of it – a bus station, a railway station, Law Courts, and a palace (which is uninhabited, presumably because it's falling down: given that, you have to wonder why a town council would want to draw attention to it in the first place).

But because we'd pre-booked a night in its modest parador (with its first class service at such odds with what we found outside its pleasant confines) we stayed in Calahora. Luggage stowed away, refreshing shower a pleasing experience, all bright eyed and bushy tailed we sallied out for a walk to explore what was on offer. Bearing in mind the information on the sign a couple of hundred metres away, we went with, shall we say, a certain lack of conviction.

We stopped in a town centre bar for a glass of the local brew – none other than La Rioja's world famous Rioja Red – and asked the barman if he could recommend anything for us to visit. He looked at us for longer than you might have expected after setting him that particular test, blinked slowly, equally slowly looked out towards the street as if seeking help, took an age to look back at us, smiled wanly, said, rather indistinctly: "Nothing, really", and again looked out towards the street bathed in a brilliant August sun.

After a moment or two, and as much to himself as to us, he said: "I suppose there's always Rioja wine, of course." He seemed mildly pleased with himself. There was nobody else in the bar.

Dejected, we went back to the parador via the pleasant Alameda, with its gardens and flowers and pathways and shaded benches, found a quiet and cool sitting room, and read James Lee Burke until it was time to go up to our rooms for another nice shower prior to dinner.

The next morning, we set out for Haro. Geographically speaking, just about qualifying as being in the Region of La Rioja, this town of about twelve thousand souls is in the north-western-most tip, within spitting distance of the Province of Álava.

And – wait for it! – it was the very first town in the whole of Spain with electric lighting in all its streets. That happy event took place in 1890, and to this day Haro is chuffed unto its very gutties with that reflected glory.

But if there's one thing that beats electric light in this neck of the woods it's being able to call yourself 'Haro: Capital del Rioja', which, in this instance, refers to its greatest produce: to wit, wine. To my knowledge, which is admittedly limited, nobody has put a figure on it, but it must produce millions of bottles of the beautiful stuff every year. It's known principally for its red wine, of course – what the local Chamber of Commerce calls its 'motor económica' – but its whites and 'rosados' are famous, too. Yet, such fame has not been without its problems.

In 1901 and 1902, phylloxera attacked the vines and virtually destroyed them, and, with them, the whole wine industry of the Rioja Region in general, and, specifically, here in Haro. Aware of their lack of alternatives, the wine growers and their workers set to it, rolled up their sleeves, and applied themselves to the daunting (ultimately successful) task of planting vines with a greater durability and resistance to pests.

The second problem was that Haro fell out with Logroño, the administrative capital of the region. Little Haro proclaimed itself – still does, in fact, in spite of Logroño's dissatisfaction with the whole matter – not merely the aforementioned 'Capital del Rioja' but 'Costa del Vino'. Well, there's been hell to pay, I can tell you. Matters are still unresolved, and lofty Logroño's pride continues to be hurt, not that Haro seems to care about it too much: what's it got to lose, when you think about it?

Haro itself isn't a bad little town, either. Like many small towns the length and breadth of the Peninsula, it was once completely walled for obvious defensive reasons, and two of its original three gates still survive, though not in their original form, you'll understand. It's got half a dozen and more seventeenth and eighteenth century palaces and noble houses of passing interest. What Spanish town hasn't, you'll quip. It's also got the Basílica de Nuestra Señora de la Vega, begun in the tenth century, the present one dating from 1703. And just off the Main Square, it's got a cracker of a church called La Iglesia de Santo Tomás, its main door well worth a photograph or two for the album. We went there to drool.

The bugger was locked, and this in spite of the fact that we were there on the numerous occasions when the notice professed it to be open to the public. I stood there with my best pout on my face, tutting and sighing audibly and drawing glances from passers-by to the fact that I was thoroughly miffed. You come all this way and what happens, your whole body tells them. I suppose I should be more than accustomed to it by now. Unfortunately, it's not an exception.

Kicking stones and passing cats and dogs and pram-bound babies and uttering imprecations, we went and sat in the nearby Plaza de la Paz, sometimes known as the Plaza de la Constitución, always known as the Main Square. (Ahem. I've been told to specify that the stone- and cat- and dog- and baby-kicking were done by me, not her!)

In the centre of this thoroughly unostentatious but pleasant square, there's an ornate band-stand, kids on foot and on bicycles careering around its base in a manner Spanish kids do particularly well. On benches, watching, sit the elderly, with time on their hands and nothing to do with it, talking tripe to each other, shouting a croaked greeting with a cigarette-ruined voice. But it's nice to sit and people-watch and thank God for bringing you to a fairly anonymous little town like Haro, with nothing to do but watch the world go by. It beats the hell out of teaching the fifth form for the last two periods of Friday afternoon, I can assure you!

And if you're here or hereabouts on June 29, you can join the locals in the Batalla del Vino. For some unexplained reason, they'll insist you come dressed head to foot in white, a red sash around your middle, an equally red neckerchief loosely tied at your throat. Come and join this crowd on the way up to the little hermitage on the Cliffs of Bilibio on the edge of town. They're all talking to and at each other, laughing and pushing and joking. They've got water pistols and buckets and plastic containers of every shape and size, and that fellow over there's got a spray gun his mother uses for weed-killing in her vegetable patch. Someone who seems to be (nominally) in charge plants the town's flag, which he's just carried up the hill, next to the shrine.

And everyone makes their way with seemingly increased noise down to the Main Square, where every conceivable receptacle is filled with red wine, which is then thrown at or fired at or dropped on whoever happens to be near. It goes on and on until everybody's now wearing a deep pink shirt and deep pink trousers and an inane smile. Nobody gets angry or hurt, and they all go home to tell their mums and dads and wives and husbands and kids what a great time they've had.

Meanwhile, unseen and all-seeing, a diversion of the Road to Santiago meets up with the more official Road into nearby Santo Domingo de la Calzada, and we make our way towards Reinosa of Blessed Memory.

9. The first time

I'll be honest with you (you wouldn't expect otherwise, would you?): what follows is in no way an up-to-date account or description of Irún. How could it be, when the two occasions I've passed through this border town were some fifteen years apart, and the last visit – if that's what you could call it, stretching the truth to breaking point – was all but forty years ago (with a football team from The Thomas Boteler Grammar School, Warrington, in 1973)!

No, these are recollections of a 'first time', of long ago and far away (and much happiness and good fortune in between, thank God), and you seldom forget a first time in any human experience, though it may be layered with legend and, perhaps, a certain few 'inaccuracies' and embellishments which might just become acceptable to the charitable Reader or Listener.

Ever since I'd been arbitrarily rejected at De La Salle Grammar School, Carr Lane East, Liverpool 11, for inclusion in the French class – deemed not academically good enough on the basis of examination results at the end of my first, very difficult, year there – and dumped into the Spanish class with all the other down-belows, I'd embraced Spanish with an inexplicable vigour. I had no pedigree whatsoever in its direction.

I was twelve, going on thirteen, so immature it was embarrassing, but Spanish (and playing outside-left in the yellow and white hoops of the school's football team run by Brother Joseph) fed a need, whatever it was. Football I played as if it were a weekly war of attrition with other schools, as if I were somehow trying to prove a point and ingratiate myself with my fellow students and teachers, and in a manner which nowadays would have undoubtedly had me in some sort of juvenile detention centre. Spanish was the proverbial duck-to-water situation.

And all this, I might add, in spite of the excessive importance given to the acquisition of vocabulary learning and grammatical accuracy – verbal communication never entered into it, not even on the most fundamental level – and a teacher who taught by instilling naked fear of failure. I loved every minute of it.

I read voraciously about fictitious Pablo and Rosita and their life and family in real-life Cercedilla; learned and retained an incredible amount of vocabulary Spaniards would seldom use in daily situations (words for birds and plants and architectural minutiae); could translate paragraph after paragraph of English into Spanish with formidable accuracy, though the subjunctive was to remain a mystery to me for years thereafter; fancied myself a sneering matador, capable of incredible feats of daring (and even wrote a short poem in Spanish called 'La Corrida de Toros', which my teacher told me didn't scan); wrote to Real Madrid for a football programme commemorating their encounter with Manchester United, and got a reply, to boot, yellowed now and held together by crisp, almost spent, sticky tape, dated '4 de abril de 1.957', and signed by 'Antonio Calderón Hernández: El Gerente', the General Manager of the greatest football team in the world, still a treasured possession and shown to anyone showing even the most minimal interest; read 'Semana' every week in the school library, surreptitiously easing out the centre-fold of the team-of-the-week, sticking it on the bedroom wall of number 63, Otway Street, Garston, Liverpool 19; idolised Alfredo di Stéfano and Ferenc Puskas; drooled over the poetry of Gustavo Adolfo Bécquer, fancying myself equally unlucky in love and a Romantic hero, doomed to unrequited love, but worthy of admiration, in spite of that; was inordinately grateful to my unnaturally aggressive Spanish teacher for having unwittingly introduced me to this exotic world, whose involvement happily remains with me fifty years later, and to Bartomeu Barceló Roig, who, indirectly, got me to know Irún, however fleetingly.

I'd left Man Island on Liverpool's Pier Head almost two days previously, my Father seeing me onto the bus, me in school uniform, the 'Irish' suitcase in reasonable condition, sandwiches sufficient to last a regiment a week or more. If he gave me any last minute advice I can't remember. My Mother had probably told me, seeing me off on Banks Road at the 80 bus stop, to 'be careful crossing Penny Lane, now'. For my Mother, Penny Lane was synonymous with potential danger, whatever the location.

Eight long hours later – no motorways then of any consequence, don't forget, except the now long-forgotten Preston Bypass – I was in London, then on to Dover and the Cross Channel Ferry. I remember coming down the ramp in Calais after an uneventful sea journey, crossing railway lines, boarding the train for Paris, following those in front of me who, unlike me, seemed to know what they were doing and where they were going. Next stop – somehow – Gare du Nord to Gare d'Austerlitz (and the brush with a wufter) where I used appalling French to ask the engine driver if 'this train goes to Irún'. I didn't understand what seemed an unnecessarily long answer delivered with the hint of a Gallic sneer, but I got on. More than twelve long hours through the long French night, sleeping in the corridor most of the time. Believe it or not, but my ticket entitled me to travel on the train: a seat cost more! My Father hadn't bargained for that. It was enough for him that I was off to meet Bartomeu in Madrid.

And then, eventually, Irún. A boundless acreage of countless railway tracks, joining and crossing and separating and re-joining, spaghetti junction long before the term was coined, low platforms going on for what seemed miles. Slowing train and pushing and shoving in narrow corridors, still half asleep or bleary-eyed, trying to get to the doors, windows rolled down to pass out cases and bundles and packages. The open door, the high step, the platform unnaturally far below. The excitement of it all.

People walking and hurrying and running in all directions, cannoning off each other, sharp words in the dawn air after a largely sleepless night. Bags and suitcases and bundles of all sizes and vintages, porters snatching them from the hands of bleary-eyed travellers, taking them places they didn't necessarily want to go. Trolleys piled high, swaying and looking ready to topple and fall. People shouting 'gang way', or whatever they say in French and Spanish (or maybe it was Basque).

The once well dressed in rumpled suits and trilbies and creased frocks. Little old Basques in old Basque berets the size of bin lids, and weeks-old stubble, leathered faces after a lifetime in the sun and rain and wind and cold, their meagre possessions rolled under their armpits. Ages old jackets, soiled trousers, booted feet.

And the smells. Not French smells. Not the smells of Paris or Gare du Nord or Gare d'Austerlitz, not relatively recognisable smells, but utterly different smells that could then – and for another thirty years or more – only be Spanish smells. Of toilets seldom successfully flushed and drains backed up and somewhere overflowing, and pungent cigarette and cheap cigar smoke, and unseen coffee with the colour and consistency of tar and a flavour of its own that left you shell-shocked. The smells Gerard remarked on as late as 1993 when we got off the plane and into the terminal buildings of Madrid's Barajas on our personal odyssey that summer (by bus here, there and everywhere, never a wrong word between us, never the slightest misunderstanding between once-teacher and once-student: precious memories, still taken out and dusted and savoured). Spanish smells, wafted on the slight breeze of that July dawn in 1960 in Franco's Spain. 'Spain is different' was the then original logo dreamt up by the infant Spanish Tourist Industry under Fraga Iribarne, and how right they were, though not necessarily in the way they'd meant.

Just as soon as we'd been told to get off the train in French Hendaye to walk the hundred metres or so across the International Bridge over the Bidasoa, we'd boarded another train to take us the insignificant distance to nearby Irún. Immediately you became aware, without being told, that Spain was indeed different. More basic, more visibly backward, more mysterious than the gentler France we'd left minutes ago.

And – no fault of this humble scribe, either – different in ways almost impossible to describe. You felt it. It was there all around you and you breathed it in and out and moved in it and lived within it. In the lifeless eyes of the pair of Guardia Civil, in their funny hats and their not so funny guns strapped to well-fed stomachs; the unshaven, sullen ticket inspector who was used to all this travelling and you weren't; black dressed women of indeterminate but advanced age, baskets on each arm, faces with the wrinkles of years of a hard life behind them; barmen and waiters in the station's bar-cum-café, silent, except for looks that spoke volumes, brisk in their movements.

Irún, battered and bombarded from land and sea and air in late August, 1936, little more than a month after the start of the Spanish Civil War. Machine guns and heavy artillery and armoured cars and hand to hand fighting. Positions gained and lost and regained, and people caught in the cross-fire, others summarily executed (on both sides), others leaping into the Bidasoa and swimming to France and exile and safety. Almost the whole of the civilian population crossing the International Bridge on the road to safety and French Hendaye.

On foot, by wheelchair, by horse and cart, animals and terrified children and refugees with their few, broken, pathetic belongings piled high and precariously on horse-drawn and hand-pushed carts. In panic and tears and penniless, the town in flames behind them. Franco's innocent victims. Collateral damage, we'd coldly call it now. Broken lives and scattered families and naked fear and utter incomprehension and ignorance of when and where it would all end. Franco: the bastard.

I never went into the town, of course. Even if I'd wanted to go, the train wouldn't have waited for me to satisfy what little curiosity I might have had about this town of thirty thousand inhabitants (which has now doubled that figure). By dint of its geographical position, it was then, and still is, a place of some considerable importance in travelling from one place to another, still a southwards passage from France into European

Spain, still a crossing-place.

I do remember feeling dirty and in need of a wash and a wee, going into the station toilets, assailed by the overpowering smell, and deciding I no longer needed a wash that badly. I did have a wee, though, wincing and holding my breath. I bought a bottle of water – carbonated, I later found out, when it exploded when I opened it somewhere near Burgos later that morning. I hauled my case on board the train, sat on the floor of the carriage with my legs dangling out of the open door, sawing the stifling heat, ate my Mother's sandwiches, now curled like parchment, and watched Irún disappear as the sun came up.

Next stop, fifteen seemingly endless hours away, Estación del Norte, Madrid, a world away.

10. Southern discomfort

How do you – how does one – come to form an opinion of a place visited? What's the procedure, if any such thing exists? Surely it's got to be the tried and tested 'first impressions', whatever the other yardsticks may be. And, in our experience, it has just as much to do with the people you meet and the intimacies granted or achieved.

Nobody, surely to God, can doubt that positive impressions are immediate and instantaneous when you see Salamanca or Sevilla or Toledo for the first time. Approach the Roman Bridge crossing the Tormes and you realise there and then that so much awaits you to be explored and enjoyed in Salamanca, and not just the major monuments, either. Do the same in Sevilla as you drive across one of the bridges over the Guadalquivir, and you sense something palpably different, a new world to explore. And who could remain unaffected by the approach to Toledo, sitting majestically above the Tajo, which cleaves its way around the lower slopes of rocky outcrop, this city so immortalised in Spain's history and culture?

Then, in another category, perhaps, there are places like Puebla de Sanabria and Toro and Villafranca del Bierzo, little known except to their circles of friends and admirers. On your first visit, you know there's something of enduring worth there, even if you can't put your finger on it straightaway. There's a pulse there, and if you give it just a little time, allow it to work on you, you'll feel it more and more with each passing visit. That's what happened to us two.

All three of them we came across purely by accident (and good fortune) rather than by design, out of the need to break a lengthy journey started in the early evening from Madrid's Barajas. We remember the people there, and they remember us, recognise us each time we return, and that's gratifying: the refreshingly open, enthusiastic Ana Galindo Lobato in Puebla de Sanabria; the elegantly mannered young lady on the reception desk in Villafranca's homely parador, and the chubby waitresses in Mesón Nacho five minutes away, short on words, looks that speak volumes; the owner and the head waiter and the reception staff in Toro's Hotel Juan II, with its peerless view high above the dog-legging Duero.

Then, there's Benavente, its outskirts and approaches defined by hundreds upon hundreds of tractors and combine harvesters and every conceivable type of agricultural machinery, its urban centre, when you find it, modest in the extreme. And Mieres, cold and unwelcoming and dank, grey, even on a sunny day. And don't get me going again on Verín: we're still at a loss as to what makes it tick, if, indeed, it ticks at all. To us, it's always seemed moribund at best, and a place we diligently avoid. We stayed there twice and failed to detect a heart-beat.

As for Jaén, well, the best I can say is that the jury's out at the moment, since our first visit, our first impressions, in the broiling heat of an Andalusian summer, were, shall we say, a little underwhelming.

I suppose we'd gone for a variety of reasons: we didn't know the south of Spain too well – still don't, if the truth be known – and we wanted to work positively on that perception. I liked the name, for no reason that makes any sense: I've always been a sucker for strangely named places. But, more to the point, we'd been spending a few days in nearby Baeza and Úbeda, and Jaén was only marginally out of the way on our journey back to Madrid's Barajas.

Originally, it was called Jayyan, no great leap to its present name, and it's south-west of the centre of the province of the same name, deep in Andalucía, fifty-odd miles north of Granada, both Córdoba and Sevilla to the west. It's sizeable, too, with a population approaching one hundred and twenty thousand people. And it's the number-one olive oil producer in the whole world: 'capital mundial del aceite de oliva', as it correctly advertises itself.

And this is, without a doubt, the single, most enduring memory of Jaén for the traveller. From whichever direction you approach, you're aware that you're a mere dot in the apparent infinity of olive trees marching inexorably in file across hill and mountain and valley and plain in a bewildering and constantly changing pattern which seems to owe as much to a human, guiding hand as to Nature's caprice, disappearing in the heat haze of the rocky, intimidating Jabalcuz mountains, wave upon wave advancing like battalions to the glowering Sierra Mágina.

But the cultivation of olives has not always been pre-eminent in Jaén's history. The Moors – a convenient word for a cross section of tribes and peoples of warlike Arab descent from North Africa – came here in the first decade or so of the eighth century, bent on furthering their power and scale of conquest. Like a tsunami, they spread to and conquered all parts of Spain (with the exception of the far north-west), and though their initial impulse was partially checked, Spain was effectively a Muslim-conquered country as late as the year 910, except for distant Galicia, shrouded in its mists, mountainous, inaccessible Asturias, present-day Cantabria, dominated by the Picos de Europa, and the Basque Country. The Moors thought the Basques were 'a people like beasts'. Well, now, there's a thing.

As the conquerors became settled and self-satisfied and effete and prone to internal squabbling and strife and jealousies, Jaén, along with other towns and cities in the southern half of Spain, became way-stations and Christian bulwarks against the invaders, who, little by little, concentrated their sphere of influence around Granada and Córdoba for the next five hundred years or so. Moorish and Christian borders ebbed and flowed with bewildering ease, wars between them became intermittent and inconclusive, thanks to the fact that both parties were riven with internal strife and jealousies and worldly ambition, the Christians no less than the Moors.

Jaén's most important sight bears witness to these historical vicissitudes. It's the Santa Catalina Castle, once a Moorish fortress, extended and improved by the Christians under Fernando III of Castilla, lying like a long lizard across the whole extent of the Santa Catalina Hill. It dominates and dwarfs everything, not just the sprawling city of Jaén, scattered somewhat clumsily at its feet, but the whole countryside as far as the eye can see.

Inside, it's a stunningly atmospheric, stunningly beautiful parador (the best sited in all Spain, along with Siguenza and Oropesa, perhaps?). Outside, its walls and towers and keep and battlements and courtyards are suitably discouraging to any would-be attacker, like any good castle should be. Stay anywhere in the city and it rears up menacingly, glowering down, impregnable, foreboding, enormously impressive. And, did you know, that no less a true celebrity than the very great General Charles de Gaulle wrote his memoirs here? It's true, every word of it! And what a view he must have had!

We decided to go there for coffee and a bite to eat, and to have a look around. We eventually found the road to (arguably) Jaén's premier monument. As you might expect, given the geographical location of the castle-parador, it was a winding road, almost single track, which twisted back on itself time without number. As you might not expect, the road surface was rutted, at best, and we bounced along, trying to avoid the pot-holes, wondering why a city would allow the approach-road to its most prestigious monument fall into such decay. And it wasn't just here, either.

We're all for local colour and the preservation of original landmarks, even if they've necessarily become a bit frayed-at-the-edges over time, and we were more than keen to see the cathedral, which we'd glimpsed in photographs.

It's a majestic, four-square pile, the 'bella desconocida' (undiscovered beauty), perhaps 'the most harmonious and complete of all Spain's Renaissance cathedrals', according to the publicity, which leaves me wondering just that little bit why it's never – no, never – mentioned or even whispered in the same breath as the cathedrals of León and Burgos and Santiago and Toledo and Salamanca and Segovia and Sevilla. Why is it that few people outside Andalucía – outside Jaén, perhaps – are aware of its existence?

It's eminently possible that it's 'an awe inspiring structure', and we don't for a second doubt that it's got no fewer than sixteen side chapels, all with a character and quality of their own.

But we simply couldn't find the cathedral in the heat of that Andalusian mid-afternoon! Honest to God! We couldn't find the bloody thing, try though we might as we attempted to navigate one-way streets cluttered with cars and wrecks of every vintage, parked, if such is the correct word, with complete lack of the most minimal care and attention.

Beautiful photographs show romantically narrow, steep streets of enormous character, the width of a single car, dipping and diving this way and that in all sorts of endearing manners. The reality is different. Two and, sometimes, three cars were left alongside each other, abandoned, almost, making it almost impossible for a pedestrian to make headway, never mind another vehicle.

The road surface was pitted and rutted and pock-marked, and monster, overflowing wheelie-bins obstructed pedestrian and car driver alike. There was litter everywhere, blown about sluggishly in the hot wind. We were heartily disappointed – nay, fed up unto the very back teeth – that a city which purported to offer so much in the way of convents, aristocratic palaces, churches of merit by the score, should be apparently satisfied with such an unsatisfactory presentation of its self-proclaimed (and undoubted) treasures.

We came away in a state of profound disappointment bordering on anger, with the opinion, based on what we had seen, that Jaén has been allowed to grow and develop randomly and of its own anarchic volition, rather than being the result of minimal planning. And that's a shame, and it's shameful, because even if our opinions are unique – and I'm not sure that that's the case – the city of Jaén's historical pedigree should never – never – allow even the possibility of misconception on the part of the visitor.

Maybe Jaén was having a bad day. Maybe we were having a bad day. Whatever the case, I refuse to believe, ever the optimist, that what we saw is a true reflection of this Andalusian city. In this spirit, we'll give it another go sometime soon. That's the best I can say. Sorry, Mónica from Arcade.

11. The Four K's

When Catherine first started teaching English with such unexpected success to the natives of Arcade and Ponte Caldelas in the summer of 2009, she bought herself a dictionary of such size that it had to be sent by special delivery in a customised lorry previously used for the transportation of stone blocks cut from a nearby quarry.

The Oxford Spanish Dictionary has just short of two thousand (very) tightly packed pages. As you might expect, not all the letters have even remotely the same number of words. Take the letter 'M', for instance: it's got 150 pages of tightly packed Spanish words. The letters 'W' and 'X' barely share a single page. Like these two, 'K' is not really a letter of the Spanish alphabet, in the strictest sense, although it briefly appears. Her dictionary, under 'K', lists words like the following:

> *Karting*
>
> *Kayak*
>
> *Kerosene*
>
> *Kilo (in its various appearances)*
>
> *Kimono*
>
> *Kiwi*
>
> *Knock-out*
>
> *Kodak (any kind of small camera)*

So you won't be surprised to learn from CEPSA's 'Mapamax' that there are only four places on the map of Spain which begin with the letter 'K', that they're all in the Basque Country, and that the words themselves are from the Basque language, which bears not the slightest resemblance to any known language, living or dead never mind Spanish.

Karkamu is in the Basque province of Álava, kilometres from anywhere, and not all that far from the western edge of the Pyrenees. At the last count, it had thirty – yes, thirty: not a misprint – inhabitants.

Then there's Korres, also in Álava province, which is apparently more of an indeterminate area than a single site, where outward bounders and others of similar persuasions are wont to pass their free time, walking and hiking and skiing and generally exercising in the fresh air.

Kortezui, in the Basque province of Vicaya, is absolutely huge in comparison, with no fewer than 400-plus inhabitants. Its post code, if you should choose to send a letter thither, is 48315, though why you'd want to is likely to remain a mystery. But it might just brighten the life of a native or two.

And, finally, there's Kripan, population 195. As with the previously named places, Kripan is a rural, agricultural little outpost. Strangely enough, though still geographically very much inside the Basque province of Álava, most of its inhabitants speak Castilian as the language of daily use (which won't endear them to ETA or other Basques, one would think). And, believe it or not, it has its own web site. This consists of a single photograph of half a dozen boulders of irregular size enclosing a small grassy patch. Very nice, what there is of it.

All four places – it's hard to know what to call them, really: even 'village' is a bit presumptuous – are spelt with a 'C' in Castilian Spanish, rather than the given spellings above.

Don't you think I've done rather well to have spread so little available information over two (incomplete) pages (and five hundred plus words)!

12. Bartomeu

I first met him in the summer of 1959. Like all summers of long ago, selective memory recalls them as endless days of sun and cloudless skies. The very distinct probability, of course, was that they were nothing of the sort, but at this stage of life I'm loath to set aside pleasant memories, authentic or otherwise.

He was playing tennis, loudly and excitedly, punishing the balls and the net and the court beyond the trees, initially out of sight. Willie Devine and I followed the shouts and exclamations.

He was a short, stocky, well proportioned man, not yet forty years of age, with tight, black, slightly curly hair, black rimmed spectacles, fine teeth, a flashing smile (especially the flashing smile). I remember him quite clearly, but not his playing companion, a man of apparently similar age.

His name was – and still is! – Bartomeu Barceló Roig, and he was and still is a Mallorcan Catholic priest of the Spanish Order of Missioners Sagrats Cors. He was on holiday, staying in Blackrock College, at the top of Booterstown Avenue, south of Dublin, and on the following week he would be going back to Madrid. He said he'd break his journey in Liverpool and had every expectation of taking me with him, thereafter to the Seminary in Lluc, in Mallorca's mountainous north-west.

We managed to convince him that such a transfer was not immediately possible, since the new academic year at De La Salle Grammar School, on Carr Lane East, Liverpool 11, was to start within a couple of weeks, and Brother John would not take too kindly to such a sudden change in plans. But we did agree that I'd go to Madrid the following summer (taking more than two days to get there by bus and boat and train after train, starting at Liverpool's Pier Head). I stayed with him in Calle Virgen de la Fuencisla, Barrio de la Concepción, for the better part of three weeks. He took me to Toledo and we swam – he swam, I paddled and splashed about – in the Tagus. The summer after that, I eventually went to Lluc after Bartomeu's countless invitations throughout the previous many months.

I'd been working in the Wages Office, with Fred and the rest of them, in The Garston Bottle Works – it was my second stint there – over the long summer of 1961, and I was getting a bit fed up with its familiarity and sameness. If the truth be known, the novelty had lost its allure the second time around.

I sent Bartomeu a letter to say I'd like to take up his invitation to come. Then another letter, and yet another, none of them getting a reply. Apparently (and unknown to me) he was in Madrid, and somebody in the Seminary in Lluc decided any mail could await his arrival, which was imminent. Deciding to act on my own initiative, I got a flight from Manchester to Palma de Mallorca. After all, hadn't Bartomeu asked me time without number to come?

Needless to say, I'd never been to Mallorca before. The airport was tiny, my spoken Spanish was basic in the extreme – we never spoke Spanish in the Spanish lessons, of course, even though I was following the A Level GCE Course: a proper exam, by the way, not today's mickey-mouse version – so I had difficulty in making my requirements understood. Lluc, my eventual destination, was in the north-west of the island, no distance on the map, and there was only one train per day to Inca (where I would then catch a bus for Lluc).

I missed the train, though I can't remember why. I wandered around the airport all afternoon and evening, attracting strange and inquisitive glances and stares, and slept on one of the benches that night. I was used to missing trains or travelling on trains that arrived late.

Next morning, probably the worse for wear – I can't remember – I caught the slow train to Inca. Fast or slow, there was only one train to Inca, and it was full of peasants and goats and chickens and farm produce and pungent smells of garlic and 'chorizo' and cheap cigars, and the seats were made of slats of wood. I don't recall how long it took, but the journey seemed to go on for hours and hours, twisting and winding and grinding along, blowing back smoke and ashes and grit through the open windows. At least it partially masked some of the smells within the compartment.

Fortunately – it had nothing to do with forward planning on my part – the bus from Inca to Lluc, the only one of the day, was programmed to wait for the arrival of the train. The only difference between train and bus was that one ran on twisting rails, the other on impossibly winding roads which seemed to go round and round and make little progress. The passengers and the smells were common to both, though I have to say I didn't find them overly unpleasant.

The scenery was everywhere breathtaking, mainly because the bus's wheels, teetering on the edges of badly rutted roads, did indeed take my breath away. In all probability, and out of necessity, I changed my undercrackers at journey's end.

But Bartomeu wasn't there. I was later told he'd stayed longer than anticipated in Madrid – remember, he knew nothing of my visit! – so when the bus wheezed to a stop in clouds of dust in front of a large, religious-looking building, there was nobody to meet me. Here we go again: hadn't exactly the same thing happened to me two summers previously when I arrived in Madrid's Estación del Norte just after midnight!

My only alternative was to ring the bell. Some minutes later, one leaf of the big door opened. I explained in extremely basic, halting Spanish (learned from my 'Principios de Español', Books One and Two, which I still remembered) the reason why I was standing there, school blazer in one hand, battered suitcase in the other. I was told (I think!) to wait.

Half an hour later, an ascetic-looking priest in a black soutane to his sandaled feet came and asked me rather distantly what I wanted.

("Erm. One suitcase, dishevelled appearance, middle of nowhere? What do you think I want? No prizes for guessing correctly!")

Sitting there in anticipation, I'd had plenty of time to programme a little speech which approximated to Castilian Spanish. I told him Father Bartomeu Barceló Roig had invited me to stay for three weeks. He told me, a little too coldly, I thought, that he knew of no such arrangement. Having exhausted everything I could say in Spanish and not being prepared for anything approaching a negative outcome, I suppose I must have smiled inanely. I can't say I was impressed with his version of Christian charity.

"Well, you'd better come this way, then," seemed to be what he was saying, to judge more by his body language than his actual words, all of which were lost on me. I was tired, too, and concentration was difficult to come by after my adventures of the last twenty-four hours.

On the following day, as fortune would have it, Bartomeu Barceló Roig arrived, to be greeted by one and all in the seminary: priests, students for the priesthood of every age, domestic staff. He was, most evidently, a man who inspired respect and admiration. God be praised!

He grasped me roughly to his bosom, and I knew then what the Prodigal Son must have felt. He fed me, took me upstairs to a simple room, showed me around the seminary, looked after me like a brother. He convinced me I could 'teach' English to the seminarians, and me only sixteen! Along with dozens of students, hanging on his every word, he took me walking and climbing (and sweating profusely) in the rugged Serra de Tramuntana, and along endless country lanes. On the back of his Vespa, he took me to Pollensa and Sóller and Andratx and Palma; then across to Manacor and Portocristo and Can Picafort and Alcudia, taking me to see his mother somewhere along the way.

Impossibly tortuous roads and tracks, twisting and turning and climbing and (it seemed) free-falling. Gorges and sudden peaks and terrifying drops on either side of the road. Blinding sun and blessed shade, and breathless heat in spite of the onward movement. White houses dotted randomly on the mountain slopes. Flocks of sheep and wandering, bawling cows. Horse and cart, and the odd decrepit car spraying stones and blinding dust in its crazy wake. And a sixteen year old English boy with his arms locked around Bartomeu's waist as he drove one handed, the other gesticulating to point out places of interest and memory, or to greet people in the wind-blown, sun-blasted villages we clattered through. Just about everybody knew him.

The seminary – the Santuario de Lluc – was Lluc, and Lluc was the seminary. Apart from that I can only remember one bar, to the left as you approached the building, a few tables and chairs randomly scattered under an arbour of vines, a blaring black-and-white television, and a few mesmerised locals. I think there was what passed for a general store alongside – on a very, very minor scale, you understand – which was a chemists and a post office and anything else you wanted it to be. There was one bus a day, one postal collection and delivery per week, cold water in the showers and wash basins in the seminary's rooms (no penance in the summer heat!), Spanish food which had little or nothing in common with English food. And it was unremittingly hot. That was Lluc in the early 1960s.

Pause for a moment and consider this: a sophisticated (Ha! As if!) English youth of just sixteen summers with little experience of life beyond his native Liverpool (apart from two stifling weeks in Madrid two years previously). Three weeks in another land – in another world, even! – where time had stood still and where life and progress were measured in a totally different manner. I actually prayed quite a lot in the seminary's chapel: I don't know whether it was in thanks for favours received, or asking for help to come to terms with a world way beyond my understanding and experience.

Fear not, young man! Bartomeu Barceló Roig was there and everybody loved him and he loved everybody, and I loved him, and I got to love them, and he looked after me. He didn't coddle me or favour me, but he did look after me, God bless him.

I went back to England three weeks later, kept in touch with him by letter, went to meet him in Lime Street Station in the summer of 1967.

Waited and waited and eventually went home to Otway Street, Garston, Liverpool 19. He'd phoned Eileen, the only phone in the street, saying he'd been called back urgently to Madrid, he was sorry for any trouble caused.

We continued to write to each other for a few more years, and then we lost touch. I can't explain how or why, but I always remembered him with affection, and in my prayers. I went to teach with the Jesuits of Saint Francis Xavier's College in leafy Woolton, Liverpool 25, where I stayed for six wonderful years.

It was February half term, 2002, and we two were looking for somewhere to go for a few days, to say that we'd done something with the free week other than stay at home working on school chores. The weather in flat Formby was characteristically appalling, even for February (and even for Formby), and we were both thoroughly fed up and in need of a change of scene. So, on a whim, looking through much maligned Easyjet's page, we saw the cheapest of cheap flights (even after we'd added in the carefully hidden extras) to Palma de Mallorca. It wasn't by any means what we would have chosen if there'd been a better alternative, so we booked the flight, and, independently – I'm not as soft as I look, you know – a hotel for three days in Sóller.

Mallorca's weather was as shitty as Formby's, but we'd made the choice, hired a car for three days, and might see something new. On a further whim, and with nothing planned, we drove in a north westerly direction towards Lluc. When we got there, of course, I didn't recognise it.

It was all so very much bigger than I remembered it some forty years previously. In spite of the weather, there were dozens of private cars and coaches and visitors and pilgrims in plastic macks and hoods and umbrellas. Lluc is, after all, the spiritual centre of the island, but I was unprepared for its very clear popularity. In the 1960s, it was, in the very nicest possible way, a religious backwater, though perhaps 'haven' would be a more appropriate word.

And it's amazing that a place like this should continue to exist (nay, should continue to thrive) in an island which has been much altered by the tourist explosion of the last fifty years. Think of the mindless millions who've crowded the streets of Palma and other towns over the many years with their antisocial culture – surely a contradiction in terms! – their drinking and generally boorish behaviour which shames Britain abroad. I wonder how many of them ever get to see Palma's truly magnificent cathedral!

Gardens and paths and walkways were all tastefully laid out and maintained, and even in the steady rain it was hard, after the initial shock, not to appreciate it. We went inside the Santuario, walked its halls and corridors and passageways in a daze, went into the chapel for a quick prayer, me knowledgably pointing out things I thought I remembered from long ago. I didn't remember them, which was increasingly self evident from my open mouth and gawking eyes, but I pretended I did. Otherwise, I'd have looked a bit of a fool (and we wouldn't want that, would I!).

With memories, authentic and imagined, crashing and colliding before my very eyes, we were about to leave when I suggested speaking to the lady on reception. I told her that I'd last been in the Santuario in the early 1960s, how much it had changed, how impressed we were, all of which she listened to with practiced patience and a suitable reply.

"And I stayed here. Knew a Father Bartomeu Barceló Roig, lovely man. Lost touch with him years ago, unfortunately. Must be well into his late seventies if he's a day. I suppose he's … you know … I suppose by now he's …"

"He was here yesterday."

"Eh?"

"He was here yesterday. Took a group of lads hiking."

"But he must be nearly eighty."

"Still took some lads hiking. And climbing, too."

"Well, does he live here? In one of the rooms of the Santuario?"

"No, he's got a flat in Sóller. It's part of the junior school there, and he's got a flat there, him and a few other retired priests. But they don't usually go hiking and climbing like him."

Sóller? Well I'll go to the foot of our stairs!

Since there's no Spanish way of expressing things with that level of surprise with a literal translation, I just stood there and looked both stupid and flabbergasted. I do 'flabbergasted' very well, I'm told.

She gave us his address, which turned out to be little more than a five minute walk from where we were actually staying, a hotel of minimal attractiveness or warmth, cheap and fairly nasty and lifeless. Still, it was February, after all.

When we got to the school, the front door was suitably locked to random visitors, but I managed, via the intercom, and reading aloud the details of my passport, to gain entry for the two of us. One of the teachers on playtime duty told us we'd just missed 'Father Barceló', he'd just popped out for something or other. He might be back later. Then again, he might not. Did we care to wait? We did. We listened to the kids making as much noise as they possibly could: it's a characteristic of all Spanish kids, and after a while you get used to it.

Half an hour or so later, we saw a figure striding purposefully down the corridor towards us. As he got closer, it was clear who it was, in spite of the forty year delay.

"Excuse me, Father. I think we know each other."

He stopped, looked at me briefly, pointed in triumph, and said "O'Neill!" eyes alive, smiling from ear to ear, hands extended.

Well, we talked all that afternoon with an ease and familiarity as if we'd seen each other only the previous week. We went out for a very late lunch and talked more, and we left him that evening. But he's still with me, still one of my three seminal role models, still a huge influence, though he's probably unaware of that.

Bartomeu Barceló Roig, Mallorcan to the very marrow, Catholic priest, published expert on apiary (that's bees, by the way!), is most emphatically one of God's most wonderful creations. And we two know him! Praise the Lord and pass a litre bottle of Toro Tinto!

13. Midnight in Mieres

One early evening in May 1966, some months before a myopic Ben Turpin look-alike Russian referee presented the English football team with the only trophy it was ever likely to win, Fr. Anthony J. Doyle, Society of Jesus, was perceptive enough – ha! – to appoint me to my first teaching post at Saint Francis Xavier's College, Woolton, Liverpool 25, to introduce Spanish into the school's curriculum.

Naturally, Spanish came a very long way down any list of subjects of academic importance at SFX (Classics and Religion were at the very top, as you might expect), and, of course, it could only be offered to those who had a proven track record of being completely and utterly hopeless in French, which, quite clearly, was a vastly superior language on all counts.

I also taught French, if that's the correct word to use, to the entire Second Form, whose abilities went from the sublime (Gerard, Halliwell, Nigel Watts) to the ridiculous and far beyond. I can't say I liked it, but I tried not to let it show (too much).

The 'down belows', those 'chosen' to attempt Spanish, were a real handful, but I was a far bigger handful to them than they were to me. Like the British Lions under Willie John McBride, it was a case of getting my retaliation in first. After that, we got on quite well. (Terry Hynes and Joey Barnacle and one of the Loftus tribe come to mind: basically nice kids, but still a handful.) Some of them even got to like me; some made 'pleasing progress', and they all feared me to a greater or lesser extent (which is not a boast: in those days, it represented the best in teaching methodology. Those who didn't adopt it went to the wall – or, maybe, up the wall!).

Fr. Doyle, over a cup of tea after lunch, bits of which he frequently wore proudly stuck to the upper part of his black cassock, would sometimes engage me in a largely one-sided conversation.

"How's the bally Spennish, what? Tests, that's the secret. Give them lots of tests. Good for them, tests." In spite of his Oxford accent, Fr. Anthony J. Doyle, Society of Jesus, was Irish, and a formidable Classics scholar. He was also basically a nice man and let you get on with things. And he kept parents at a significant distance. After all, what could they possibly know that he didn't?

"Yes, Father. Thank you, Father."

So, with enthusiasm by the lorry-load, an in-your-face manner in the classroom, taking no prisoners, and experience severely limited to the three weeks, at the age of sixteen or so, teaching English to the Spanish seminarians in the Monasterio de Lluc in the remoter mountains of Mallorca, I set out to make my mark. The fact that, at the time of my appointment, I had yet to sit my University Finals, seemed not to worry Fr. Doyle.

"You'll be fine, just fine, I've no doubt. Tests. Give them lots of tests. Best way, don't you know."

"Yes, Father. Thank you, Father."

Four years later, I'd managed to convince an initially doubtful Paul Crossey that an overland trip to Spain with ten chosen Fifth Form lads of proven repute was an adventure worth embarking upon. That was August 1970.

We – perhaps 'I' might be more accurate: I seem to recall Paul suddenly investing me with an unsuspected organisational ability far beyond my powers – hired a stridently orange twelve-seater Ford Transit minibus from the garage next to South Liverpool's football ground, and used that as our starting point. I must tell you that the only thing you could accurately call a plan was to get to Madrid by a certain pre-booked date, and to pick up accommodation either side of that date when and where we could find it.

We had asked Fr. Duggan if he would see us off from school after celebrating Mass for us. Since he was Rector at that particular moment, he gladly agreed, only for Fr. Doyle to countermand the offer arbitrarily, saying we could meet at the Pier Head, couldn't we: a much better place, he said. Stephen Lennon's father easily convinced the Redemptorists of Bishop Eaton Monastery to see us off in prayerful fashion, for which we were grateful.

I do remember discussing our plans for the three week adventure with Paul once on the road somewhere between Liverpool and Margate, prior to catching the bowel-wrenching hovercraft to France.

"So, Paul, when d'you think you want to take a turn at the old driving, then?"

"Pardon?" Paul could fill a single word with a range of meanings.

"When d'you want to drive?"

"Drive?"

"Yes, drive. When d'you want to start? Take turns, sort of thing."

"Oh, I don't drive. I thought you knew!"

"Oh. Right. (Jesus!)." Eight hours a day, three weeks? That's … Jesus wept!

But Paul effortlessly guided us around Paris, through Rouen and Chartres and Tours, and on down to Angouleme, where Stephen Moore left his suitcase and shared everyone's shirts and trousers and socks and under-crackers until we stopped in Angouleme on the way back some two weeks later, all of us smelling just a little.

Paul spoke 1950's text book French with a certain personalised accent and managed to get us fed and watered and billeted every night, God bless him.

Once across the French border and into Spain, we spent our first night in Tolosa, north-west of Basque Pamplona, trains ceaselessly passing literally outside our hotel windows throughout the night, much to Paul's manifest delight. Somehow, on some very questionable roads, we managed to get to sweltering, oven-hot Madrid.

We stayed in Hostal Fuencarral, a rambling old building just off Gran Vía in Calle Fuencarral, ten jiggered sixteen year olds and two similarly jiggered teachers. Sitting at a pavement café in Madrid's Gran Vía, lovesick and missing her, I wrote countless letters to Margaret, drenched on an Inverness camp site with her parents and brothers. We visited Toledo (saw the Alcázar), and Segovia (saw the viaduct), and Ávila (walked the walls). Drove up past Tordesillas, though nobody remembers doing so. Parked the Transit next to the fountain in Plaza de Santo Domingo in León. Went looking for accommodation, the only night when we weren't all twelve of us under the same roof. It was great. Forty years later and ten fifty-somethings still talk about it. So do two happily retired teachers.

Thereafter, and somehow, and for some random reason now long forgotten, we drove northwards, which had always been the general 'plan', and ended up staying in Mieres, which had never figured in the 'plan'. Not for one single moment.

And in this town of some forty-four thousand inhabitants, more or less in the Principality of Asturias, a little after midnight in mid-August 1970, we did the conga around the miserable, deserted streets of Mieres, spending the next two hours or so trying to locate our hostal for the night, singing marginally ribald ditties.

One teacher, who should have known better – Paul did know better and didn't conga – and ten sixteen year olds who were quite content not to know better and to be in the company of one teacher who self evidently and shamelessly didn't seem to want to know better: what a memory!

The fact that we were (ever so slightly) the worse for wear – after a prodigious meal washed down with an equally prodigious amount of the very best Asturian cider – further complicated matters. We couldn't remember the name of the hostal (still can't!) and had only the sketchiest idea of its location, both of which were definite disadvantages. But it was a fine night, by any standards.

Next morning, after a breakfast taken in unusual silence, we walked the streets of Mieres for half an hour or so, quickly coming to the conclusion that there was absolutely nothing to detain us further. Even in mid August, it was uniformly grey and uninviting and signally lacking any detectable human warmth.

Forty years later, as Margaret and I motored northwards from Madrid where we'd left Pauline and Henry, bound for Oviedo's midget airport to pick up a group of Pax Travel People (lovely crowd), I felt the same about this town whose population has fallen from 70,000 in the 1960's to 44,000 by 2010.

Mieres has always relied exclusively on its coal mines that litter and befoul the area, and it's suffered over the years as King Coal has inexorably declined in importance; and it's always been something of a hot-bed, as they say, of revolutionary fervour over the years, never a place to bend the knee to anyone in authority, let alone centralising, worlds-away Madrid.

In 1906 and in 1917, and again in 1934, miners' rebellions were forcefully put down by the government in Madrid. On that last occasion, the Republican government of Theroux, already (almost) on its last legs, sent Francisco Franco y Bahamonde, a rising star in the Armed Forces, to quell the rebellion. With the assistance of the Spanish Foreign Legion (of mercenaries), the little man from green Galicia gave the distinct impression that he enjoyed himself immensely, an apprenticeship, perhaps, for the later roles he would gladly assume from 1936 until the bastard eventually snuffed it in November 1975.

Perhaps, here and there in some hidden corner – so well hidden that it confounds detection – Mieres has the odd something or other worth tarrying a while to see. And by the time you read this, Reader, you won't be surprised to learn that Mieres doesn't get a single mention – not even its name – in The Book's 720 pages. But I thought you might enjoy – if such is the word – these little reminiscences. They still mean something of significance to two happily retired (again!) teachers and ten fifty-somethings, who still share these memories.

In fact, you might be inclined to agree with me that the human element of this article is far more interesting than the presentation of Mieres, which, sadly, probably says all there is to say about Mieres.

14. Nacimiento del Ebro

If you've been fortunate enough – ahem! – to have read "Of Castles and Caballeros", you'll know at least a little about our thirty-odd year love affair with Reinosa (of Blessed Memory). If not – perish the thought! – then here's something of a précis to put things into some sort of context.

In mid July, 1979, three teachers from Saint Mary's College, Great Crosby, Liverpool L23 3AB (as its post code was then), took forty-five kids on the school's first ever visit to Reinosa, a small, relatively ordinary town in what was then the northerly province of Santander, and which, shortly thereafter, came to be known as the region of Cantabria, a green and pleasant land (which is not averse to variable, temperamental weather, I'll have you know). For the next twenty-five uninterrupted summers, with changes in the accompanying teachers (except for us two) at the helm for most of that period, kids from the school – firstly, all boys, then boys and girls, once the College became a mixed independent school – queued up in the first days of the September term with their twenty pounds deposit clutched in their little hot hands.

Our first accommodation, spartan in the extreme, was in the Colegio Menor de la Juventud, run on what you might euphemistically call a 'personal' level by Jesús López Íñiguez, who was endlessly attentive to our requirements. It was little more than a youth hostel during the summer months. Somehow, we managed to avoid illness in spite of the shortcomings, shall we say, in the hostel's kitchens, which were run in a most quixotic manner, and would never pass muster in this day and age. They didn't then, but that's another matter. It's actually still in operation, though not as a hostel, having been modernised over the years and now used as a school for apprentices.

After five years of that, we stayed with Isa and Verónica and Chuchi (God rest his soul) for the next twenty summers in Hotel La Casona, on what passed for the (totally invisible) border between Reinosa and Nestares. La Casona was actually no more than a couple of metres, officially, inside Nestares, so it had its own post code.

Thankfully, the kids from the very outset were a motley crew, going from the sublime to the ridiculous, the academically outstanding to those who most certainly would nowadays qualify for special-education needs (or 'thick as a brick', if you're from the old, more realistic school of teaching). But we seldom had an out-and-out 'baddie', though we had our fair share of benevolent, wonderfully pleasant nutters, and a seemingly endless number of 'characters', all of whom enriched the experience. The majority were actually studying Spanish – 'studying' being far too strong a word for many of them – so the trip was quasi educational in a distant sort of way. It was thought to be an enjoyable experience and a success by almost everyone, to judge from those who came year after year and who considered themselves 'Reinosa Veterans', a group within a group.

I suppose it's true to say that Reinosa itself was relatively limited in what it could offer demanding kids, but we teachers were a resourceful lot and kept them busy and generally satisfied throughout the two weeks' stay.

We'd take them to El Cid's Burgos for the day for a change of scene and for a bit of culture on Manolo's bus, his pride and joy, sometimes with his scary wife (who dwarfed him, which was easily done, it must be said), sometimes with his lad, who never spoke a word but just stared at you in a disconcerting way (and reminded you of the banjo playing child in the film "Deliverance").

"Now, over there, girls and boys, is the Cathedral of Burgos, one of the finest in all Spain. It was built in … Hey, this way! Where are you all going? Where are they going, Eric? Come back, you buggers, and get some culture down you!"

Or we'd go to the pleasant seaside town of San Vicente de la Barquera (where Sue climbed up to the castle every year) and then on to the white sands of Comillas for the day, doling out butties (which were usually buried surreptitiously in the sand) and fizzy drinks and sun cream.

"Now you're talking, Miss! This is more like it! Will you put some of that cream on me back, then? Me mother'll go spare if I don't come home with a bronzie on me."

"Look, Phythian, you're only supposed to bury his feet, not his entire body. Who is it you've got down there, anyway? Give us a clue."

"Miss, Sir, I've lost me thingy. I 'ad it when I dived into the water but someone must of pinched it 'cos I can't find it any more."

Then there was Aguilar de Campoó (actually in the province of nearby Palencia, an hour or so away) when the weather forecast for the beach was less than promising.

"No, there are no mountain bikes for hire for the simple reason there's no mountains hereabouts, if you've noticed. They're the big things that look like enormous rocks but a thousand times bigger. Got it now, have we?"

"Miss, when we goin' back to the hotel in ... What's the place called, Miss? Where we're staying, you know. I've forgot."

And on the way back from the beach, sand everywhere in spite of our alertness, we'd stop off for a couple of hours and enjoy the quaint charm of Santillana del Mar.

"Miss, when we goin' back to that hotel? You know, the one we're stayin' in. What's it called again?"

But every year, come rain or shine – and it always shone, if memory serves me right, except for one awful summer – we'd walk them, under increasing protest (but to no avail) the couple of kilometres from Hotel La Casona to the Nacimiento del Ebro, on the farther side of nearby Nestares.

There are probably no more than five really significant rivers amongst the eighteen hundred or so which vary from the thousand kilometre long Tajo (Tagus) to the almost countless tiny streams, many of them dry river beds for much of the year until the rains come, turning them into churning, headlong, joyous, cascading waters.

The Duero, beloved of the beloved Antonio Machado, rises in the high lands of largely undiscovered Soria province, working its twisting way inexorably westwards, past Valladolid and on through Tordesillas, dog-legging its way past Terrific Toro and on to (less terrific) Zamora, entering

Portugal at Miranda do Douro (and slightly changing its name in the process), emptying into the Atlantic in Porto. Remember it?

The Tajo, too, ends up in Portugal's Atlantic, specifically in Lisbon, flowing under the old Salazar Bridge (my first sight of Portugal back in 1965, wracked with sea-sickness, a physical shadow of my former self). Its earlier passage westwards has been through Toledo and wonderful, under-explored Extremadura, through countless dams and reservoirs, a much needed source of power and sustenance for this formerly parched region.

Further south, but starting in the high hills of Cuenca province, the Guadiana winds its way westerly into Extremadura, around battle-scared Badajoz, delving deep into Portugal's south-east corner. It, too, provides much needed water to this relatively barren area of the Iberian Peninsula.

The Guadalquivir (Wadi al-Kabir, in Arabic) is in southerly, centuries-impoverished Andalucía. It's Spain's only inland river for ocean-going traffic, spilling into the Altantic near Cádiz. In the old days, the 'Golden Age' ('golden' for more reasons than one), Spanish treasure-laden galleons from South America sailed directly into Sevilla, in no small measure the reason for that great city's greatness.

But the Ebro is different. Alone amongst Spain's great rivers, it flows from west to east, passing Logroño and Zaragoza, meeting the Mediterranean south of Tarragona. And every year for twenty-five years we took the kids there, to the very spot where it all started, and a more humble beginning you could hardly find.

(Here endeth the necessary geography lesson, you'll be more than pleased to hear! Back to the much more interesting human element in all this, eh?)

"Right. So, can everybody hear me? Anybody who can't, put your hand up. Am I keeping you awake at the back? Anybody needing to go back to the hotel for anything, say so now, because we're out for the day.

Can you lot hear me at the back? I'll start talking when you finish, okay? I don't want any soft-lad questions once we get started. Sun cream, hats, bag with a change of clothing, towel and swimming things, a few pesetas: that's all you'll need. Not much, because there's nothing to buy where we're going, except for a drink if the restaurant's open. Hang on! Just a minute! You listening to me, Jane and Jane? Or am I talking to myself again? Right. Just keep together and keep up with the rest of us. I'll walk ahead and Miss and Wigan Mr ONeil will bring up the rear. You won't want to get behind them if you know what's good for you! What?"

"Where's the bus, Sir?"

"What bus, heart of my heart? Funnily enough, in the garage. Why?"

"We walking?"

"Course we're walking. It's only five kilometres."

"Five kilometres? Five kilometres? Honest to God? That's miles!"

"It's a doddle. Wrap up and keep up."

"Miss, can I go back an' change out of these high heels, then?"

Half an hour later, we're ready to go. The picnic's in six bags to be carried at intervals along the road by the older ones, boys and girls. We've got bread and cheese and ham and chocolate and fruit, and enough water to fill a swimming pool. The day's glorious: cloudless, sunny, but not yet too hot, and the cycle path that goes from Nestares out to Fontibre is just about perfect for walking. Added to this, there's little traffic in either direction, but after ten minutes walking we're already strung out over one hundred metres, in spite of Miss and Wigan Mr ONeil's best efforts. So Jonathan companionably suggests I slow down. Five minutes later, he companionably suggests I stop as the back markers are now out of sight. Since Jonathan's an extremely sensible youth, not given to hyperbole, we stop.

Left and right, it's simply beautiful. Untouched scenery, fields upon fields of forty shades of green, gently rising and gently falling: here and there, the odd house, open for the summer, its shutters flung open; a tiny village of half a dozen houses in various states of repair; dry stone walls and healthy looking cows, watching us pass (slowly); a seemingly abandoned bus stop with a weather-worn timetable twenty years out of date; one or two cottages in ruins, rekindling a personal dream, realised many years later, though not in Cantabria; fresh air and rising temperatures; the odd car swishing by, tooting and raising dust.

We pass Argueso on the right with its partially ruined castle, still in fairly good condition considering its great age; Salces, at the crossroad, where we once ate in a converted hay loft with Isa and Chuchi (and never managed to find it again, woe is us!); Villacantid, little more than a kilometre marker at the side of the road, no clear sign of habitation; Paracuelles and Espinilla, massive in comparison, with twenty or so houses in each settlement, and the obligatory couple of bars, a barn housing Radio Reinosa where I once did a live interview.

What should have been a forty-five minute walk has now comfortably doubled in time. There's one or two moans, but, generally speaking, the troops are some way short of rebellion, especially since Miss keeps telling them that "It's just around the next bend in the road and would I lie to you, Jane?" Gullible lot. Many bends and a few lengthy straights later, the majority of them on auto pilot but still jabbering away, we turn left into a downhill side-road that leads into the tiny village of Fontibre, which eighty or so people call 'home'. It's then that we discover that Gabriela from Hightown, as comparatively fresh as a daisy, has left the bag with the chocolate in it five kilometres back in the hotel, which explains why she's as comparatively fresh as a daisy. Strike chocolate off the list, then, to a chorus of "Oh, no! Divvy!"

They swarm down the slope without knowing where they're going, a few of them slipping and tumbling to the bottom, their fall being arrested by the robust tree trunks at the stream's edge, but they're up in an instant, fanning out in all directions as if they know the place intimately, eager for brainless adventure.

Depending on the season – and we've only been there with school groups in the comparatively dry summer months: winter's a different thing in this neck of the woods, let me tell you! – at the foot of the natural amphitheatre of paths and rudimentary steps, there's a small stone obelisk a few metres into the stream, and it's more or less there that the mighty Ebro begins its long pilgrimage to the Mediterranean. This marker here is the Nacimiento del Ebro, kids! They're hanging from the obelisk, an impossible number of them, getting their photos taken, pulling faces for the camera.

This lot are scarcely interested in the geographical or historical nuances of what they see and almost immediately disregard. For them, it's just another river, and they're not what you might call overly impressed, either.

"That it, Miss? That's a river?"

"Yes, Child of Grace, that's a river, complete with water, and for your less than enquiring mind that's how all rivers start to one extent or another, a little piddle deep in the ground, on its way to greater things."

"What d'you mean, Miss?"

It gathers some slight momentum passing Reinosa (of Blessed Memory, if you recall), underneath Hotel La Casona, which was formerly a mill, eastwards and southerly on its journey to Aguilar de Campoó, jinking and dipping and diving across to Miranda de Ebro, on beyond Logroño, southeasterly, now, past Tudela and mighty Zaragoza, Caesar Augustus in times gone by, wriggling this way and that before splashing into the Mediterraean, free at last.

It's lived through the innovatory irrigational projects of the 1920's under far-seeing Calvo Sotelo (who never foresaw his own assassination on the streets of Madrid in the first days of July, 1936); witnessed the battles along its banks in the late summer of 1937; watched dispassionately one year later when Republicans and Nationalists fought the bloody campaign which came to be known as the Battle of the Ebro, which did comparatively little to resolve anything for either side.

But this mindlessly happy lot don't care one jot about such considerations, and, ultimately, why should they? They've plundered whatever food they want from the haversacks, they've roundly condemned Gabriela from Hightown for her oversight concerning the chocolate. Now they're tying each other to the trees, whooping like Apaches bent on scalping, or swinging from branch to branch making what they believe to be monkey-noises. They're walking across the rocks and into the Ebro's stream, as happy as pigs in whatever pigs are traditionally happy in.

Not for the first time, nor the last, the tiny settlement of Fontibre resounds to youthful Liverpool accents and cries of joy and pain, completely oblivious to historical considerations. Perhaps that's how Fontibre and the Nacimiento del Ebro should be remembered.

Meanwhile, Gabriela from Hightown's looking for redemption.

"Miss, Sir, I've just found this little café where they sell chocolate ice-creams, honest to God! Come an' see. It's just up here!"

We go in search of further pleasure, and thank Gabriela from Hightown, but not too effusively, you understand, just in case she should forget earlier omissions.

15. Big 'Ñ' and little 'ñ'

Believe it or not – and I'm sure you will, or you could check on its veracity yourself – but there are two spellings of the letter 'N/n' in the Spanish alphabet, and each is accorded a dictionary section of its very own. There's the normal one, 'N' or 'n', which gives us such place names as Nájera (which you almost certainly won't have heard of) and Nerja, which will probably be relatively familiar to English ears.

And then there's words starting with 'Ñ' or 'ñ', of which there are very, very few: in fact, no more than a maximum of three dozen in the entire language. That being the case, you won't be overly surprised to learn that there is only one solitary town or settlement in the whole of Spain's half a million square kilometres (almost 200,000 square miles) which begins with 'Ñ': it's called La Ñora. The squiggle over the 'Ñ/ñ', by the way, is called a 'tilde', and any word containing this letter is pronounced, nasally, as 'ny'.

The Latin (or Roman) alphabet had, with modifications here and there, twenty six letters, some of them written, quite naturally, as doubles: 'annus', for example. When the monks, frozen still and bent over their manuscripts and squinting in the poor light cast by a five watt flickering candle, painfully transcribed one vellum after another after another, one bright spark amongst them hit on the idea of a form of shorthand (economizing on paper by so doing).

Along with other double letters, Latin words containing double 'n' ('annus', for example, again) were written with a dash over one single 'n'. So, 'annus' eventually became 'año', and in time 'ñ' became a letter in its own right in the Spanish alphabet; and when the use of printing presses side-lined the monks, the practice was continued and established.

Now, to you and to me it's difficult to appreciate that this linguistic development is of any importance at all in the great scheme of things; but to Spanish speakers the world over it became a matter of national and cultural pride, to the extent that Spanish computer keyboards have a separate key for 'Ñ/ñ'. (It's actually to the right of 'L/l'.)

In 1991, that bastion of common sense supposedly working for the common good, the European Union (then known as the EEC), inadvertently unleashed a cultural war after attempting to introduce a manifestly unnecessary change of little or no value. Its pen-pushers recommended in a report (costing millions of scuds, no doubt) the repeal of the regulation preventing the sale in Spain of computer keyboards not displaying all the letters of the Spanish alphabetical system. It claimed that the Spanish stance was tantamount to a protectionist measure and, therefore, against the principles of the Free Market. Meanwhile, there's a constant economic crisis of sizeable proportions at every turn; the Greeks continue to spend more than they've got and get uppitty when it's drawn to their attention that they might just have to change their attitude: fat chance of that!; sovereign borders are deemed no longer to exist; unsustainable immigration goes unchecked, and they do bugger all about it. The shape of bananas is of far greater importance. And the Spanish letter 'Ñ/ñ'.

Well, there was hell to pay, I can tell you! The Real Academia Española (RAE) waded into the fight, claiming that such an action was a serious attempt against the official (Spanish) language.

And Gabriel García Márquez, Nobel Prize winner for literature in 1982, and a man of considerable clout in the world of words, said it was 'escandaloso' that the UE should dare even to attempt to eliminate the letter. He spoke of 'abuso' and 'arrogancia', and later celebrated in print 'el triunfo de la ñ' when the fools from the UE (with obviously nothing better to do than attempt to pass laws of not the slightest consequence) quickly backed down (but still kept their well paid jobs).

All this for thirty-odd words! Good-Jesus-Tonight!

Where were we? I got carried away and lost me place, m'Lud! Ah, yes, travels through the Spanish alphabet and La Ñora! The only place bar none in Spain beginning with 'Ñ'.

If I didn't actually pass through La Ñora in 1961, I must have come pretty close, no more than half a dozen kilometres away, at very most. I was travelling by car to Benicàssim with the architect father of Eugenio Gutiérrez López, trying to understand what he was jabbering about, opting to pretend to be asleep (shame on me! He was a very nice man.). We'd driven in a south-easterly direction from Madrid, through Aranjuez and featureless Albacete and a host of nondescript towns and villages in between. It was July and it was blazingly hot.

I remember getting to Murcia where Eugenio's father and I stayed overnight – after eating on a rooftop restaurant just after midnight – because he had some business in Murcia on the following morning. The next day he showed me around the city, but my only memory is of the cathedral, a modest pile, it seemed to me at the time. The fact is I wasn't really into cathedrals at the age of sixteen, so my appreciation may not have been all it should have been.

La Ñora, some six kilometres west of Murcia (a university town and the home to 350,000 people), is actually a municipal district of four settlements, of which this small town is by far the biggest and most important place. 'Important', by the way, is a relative term, you'll understand. You won't be surprised that its history, such as it is, goes back to Moorish Al-Andalus. In point of fact, one of its two features worthy of mention is its famous 'rueda' (waterwheel), introduced in 1408 into this initially parched but ultimately fertile corner of Spain to transport water throughout the whole area, and still doing a good job, thank you very much.

Its other monument of note is the Monasterio de San Pedro de La Ñora, built in the mid sixteenth century under the patronage and financial support of Alonso Vozmediano de Arróniz. Like many wealthy men before and since, he bequeathed lands and money on his death (in this instance, to the Order of Los Jerónimos), perhaps to make his passage to Eternal Life just that bit easier (or am I being a little uncharitable?).

A century later, after the River Segura, flowing through nearby Murcia, spectacularly burst its banks, the monastery was moved to a more geographically favourable site. It's called 'El Escorial de Murcia' after

118

Herrera's great palace-monastery of El Escorial in the centrally located Sierra de Guadarrama, built for the lugubrious Philip II (of Armada infamy). Even proud locals refer to it as having a 'severo estilo clásico' and being a 'colosal mole arquitectónico', so you have the feeling before seeing it that you won't be in for the greatest of thrills.

The whole Murcia area was colonised by Los Jerónimos, who effectively governed and administered every aspect of life, and no bad job they did, either, I'm here to tell Spanish Catholic-bashers. Thereafter, in the nineteenth century, the building had more than a varied history: it was abandoned, then became a lunatic asylum, then a hospital (especially during the 1855 cholera epidemic, and thereafter). It was sacked, became a fortress, then an arsenal, and was eventually restored.

It fell into considerable disrepute during the horrendous Spanish Civil War of 1936-1939 – what didn't! Thank you, Franco, you bastard – and was later renovated (again), this time by the Society of Jesus (the loved-hated Jesuits), who turned it into a retreat house and apprentice work-centre. It's now the Universidad Católica de San Antonio de Murcia (UCAM).

Like all Spanish towns – and especially, it seems, Andalusian towns – La Ñora is big on Holy Week processions; but since I've already expressed or intimated my (English) views on the practice of the Catholic Faith and its outward manifestations in Spain, I'll force myself not to repeat it here, which, if you think about it, is an obtuse expression of opinion in itself! Ahem.

Nowadays, the service industries, construction, and a certain amount of largely inconsequential agriculture give employment to (some of) the people of La Ñora, which, you'll correctly suspect, isn't saying an awful lot.

The truth is that you wouldn't go out of your way to stop in La Ñora for any length of time for anything more than a coffee and a wee. But since La Ñora is the only settlement in Spain beginning with 'Ñ', and this work purports to be an A to Z of travels in the country, it has to be included, hasn't it?

Thank you for your patience. Over and out.

16. The Golden Scrubbing Brush Award (2007)

We don't like big cities. Oviedo is a big city of two hundred thousand inhabitants in the Principality of Asturias. We like Oviedo (and we like Asturias, too, come to that).

The first time we went there was about fifteen years ago with Arantxa. We'd been on a day-out from Ronnie's Gijón, and we'd stopped off for lunch in Villaviciosa, just along the coast. Then it was decided (note the passive voice!) to return to Gijón and on to Oviedo, though God knows why we let ourselves be persuaded to go back to Gijón to get to Oviedo. Perhaps it was one of Arantxa's famous short-cuts, though it most clearly wasn't, we two knew for certain that it wasn't, but we allowed ourselves to be guided by her navigation: Mistake Number One, since she must surely be, and by her own admission, the worst navigator on Planet Earth.

When we eventually got to Oviedo, hours after it was humanly possible to do so, it was such an utterly drab February day that we decided to cut our losses, turn around, and head back to Gijón, accepting the whole day to have been a complete waste of time.

Mistake Number Two: we got hopelessly lost, and since Arantxa said she knew Oviedo like the back of her hand, knew a quick way out of the seemingly endless one-way streets of the city, evening prematurely drawing in, we decided to trust her judgement. Result: we 'revisited' places and landmarks we'd passed many times in the last half hour, so much so that the same people we'd continually passed waved to us in friendly fashion. To keep up appearances, we waved back, two faces with a rictus smile.

Finally deciding to do what we should have done first, and following our own intuition – as well as the traffic signs clearly on display, which Arantxa had dismissed as irrelevant and worthless – we were soon on the way back to Gijón, thoroughly pissed-off by the whole adventure, when a little voice from the back seat, in perfect if slightly accentuated English said: "I need a wee." Strangely enough, we never went back to Oviedo with Arantxa. If we found somewhere to satisfy her need, I can't recall.

The second visit was when we saw Oviedo in a different light, and got to like it. It was a bright day in April, 2009, with rather a nice group of thirty-odd Pax Travel pilgrims from the Midlands under the ever watchful eye of Canon Stephen, who had every right to have things done his way (though he was very diplomatic about almost everything). They'd flown into Asturias Airport (an embarrassingly tiny and inconsequential terminal near industrial Avilés) on the first leg of their (luxury coach and luxury hotels) pilgrimage to Santiago de Compostela, and we two were their guides.

There's a general misconception that there's only one Road to Santiago, that being the so-called French Road which starts at various points in France, crosses the Pyrenees via a number of different mountain passes, and goes on by way of Pamplona and Puente de la Reina and Burgos and León and Villafranca del Bierzo (or lugubrious Lugo). But out-of-the-way Oviedo has a rich tradition of being a highly attractive and well used alternative route to Saint James' shrine. As far back as the ninth century, this interpretation of the pilgrimage was initiated by Alfonso II at what's now called – wait for it! – the Plaza de Alfonso II, right in front of the city's impressive cathedral. There's a plaque on the pavement to celebrate the event, just in case – perish the thought! – you might doubt its veracity, which I'm sure you wouldn't, not even for a moment.

And the third time we went to Oviedo was with that lovely group of twenty-eight elderly Australians who, truth to tell, had their minds more on ultra-remote San Sebastián de Garabandal than on Oviedo. But since it was the feast of Jesus' tax-gathering apostle, Saint Matthew, and since there was more than a suggestion from Juan on the reception desk in Hotel Ciudad de Oviedo that yet another shroud rumoured to have belonged to the crucified Christ would be on show and venerated in the cathedral during the course of the midday High Mass, we decided, as a group, to attend.

At breakfast that morning, Margaret and I had arranged to meet them at the front door of the cathedral around eleven-fifteen, since, we were reliably informed, everyone in Oviedo and beyond would be attending the performance – I use the word 'performance' advisedly, you must understand – and seats would be at a premium. Desperate, not for the first time, for yet another coffee – "What is it with you two and coffee?" – we espied a bar no more than fifty metres from the cathedral. Bear the distance in mind for future contrast and comparison.

Its surface area was no more than twice the size of a modest-size living room. The walls, apparently, hadn't been painted since before the outbreak of the Spanish Civil War, and their original colour might well have been a muddy shade of ocre (or maybe that had more to do with the million or more smokers who had disgraced its shadowy interior over the last seventy years or so). It smelt like a toilet.

We ordered two coffees, which might well have been coffee. Or something else: it was hard to say. Two sluts – or, if you prefer, two female Spanish celebrities of highly dubious worth or attractiveness with faces like thoroughly smacked arses under layers of face paint – were shouting at each other on a flat screen television high on the wall in the corner. Nobody was listening, as you might expect. This is Spain – twenty-first century Spain, to boot – and noise is everything, so the unwatched television was merely fulfilling the necessary function of adding to the noise.

I went into the toilet prior to paying and leaving. It stank like what it was, which was hardly surprising since the previous occupant had forgotten to consign his offering to the drains before leaving, not unknown in this neck of the woods, I might add. There was a hole in the ceramic base and the raised design of two feet, just to give the ignorant an idea of what was expected of them. For Margaret's sake, and to avoid unexpected surprises, I popped my head into the vacant ladies' cubicle. It was identical (except that the previous occupant was obviously well bred and had pulled the chain).

Bear in mind that this is late September, 2011, that Oviedo is the cultural and commercial capital of the Principality of Asturias, that it's a university city of some national note, that there's lots of similarly colourful bars scattered around its historical centre (not all quite so basic, I hasten to add, lest you now feel disinclined to pay a visit to visit-worthy Oviedo). This one, I repeat, is no more than fifty metres from the city's impressive cathedral.

But rather than repel me – as it should, me being English, don't you know – I can only smile thinly and say "Welcome to Spain!" But, in no way disillusioned, since we'd seen it all before, we made our way to the façade of the cathedral to meet the Australians.

They weren't there! Here we go again, shades of Lisbon Airport all over again, only this time they've all disappeared, not just 'young' Robert (who's pushing forty, and, truth to tell, and being most charitable towards him, is less than worldly-wise and not all there, so to speak!). We looked wordlessly at each other. I went one way, Margaret went the other, both in a search of what was clearly a waste of time, given the thousands milling about in the Plaza de Alfonso II in front of the Cathedral of Oviedo. It wasn't as if they'd be wearing floppy hats with corks hanging from them, bearded like Rolf Harris and flexing a bow-saw, singing 'Tie me kangaroo down, sport' in unison, the better to be identified.

On a hunch – we were desperate and fast running out of ideas (and patience) by the second – Margaret forced her way through the crowds around the doors to the cathedral, and being taller than the average Spaniard-of-a-certain-age, she glimpsed them. They'd bagged the seats on the first two rows just left of centre, and had that look on them and the rigidity about their shoulders that shouted: 'We shall not be moved, cobber!' (or something like that).

Meanwhile, just behind them, one of the ushers, identified by an official badge proclaiming him to be José Antonio, was trying to eject a fiftyish strumpet dressed head to toe in vibrant orange, who, by word of mouth and digital sign-language, told him very clearly that she wasn't moving, and where he could relocate his official badge, if push came to shove.

Naturally, the Australians found this an unexpected entertainment, the more so when a flustered José Antonio returned five minutes later with two traffic policemen (one of whom was a woman), who finally had greater success. With a few choice words, Orange Strumpet, in no way fazed, giddily heaved herself upright ... and spent the rest of the Mass wedged between the choir and the official photographers on the left hand side of the Sanctuary, on what we used to call the 'Gospel Side' fifty-odd years ago.

Then the big-wigs entered, shining suits, freshly barbered and shaved, with their women (perhaps, even, their wives: you never know), making great play of where they should sit on their once-a-year attendance at Mass; television and newspaper photographers engaged in friendly bouts of pushing and shoving to get the best angles; sacristans and other minor officials appeared in various places in the Sanctuary, moving this or that item a centimetre to left or right and back again, looking with measured disdain at the good and the bad and the ugly readying themselves for the performance.

Meanwhile, expensively attired late-comers pushed their way in search of sitting or standing spaces where there was simply no room – dick-heads, the lot of them: what are you, Portuguese or something? – looking at our group and expecting them to give up their places. Naturally belligerent Mario Plazzer and his wife and fellow Australians, all bound for remote Garabandal, stared back resolutely, ready for a fight, if it came to that.

Then it was Lights! Camera (or Cameras)! Action! And dozens of doddery clerics shuffled in in twos, followed by the bishop, expensively gowned, designer bearded, flabby faced, smiling and blessing anybody and everybody. José Antonio and other officials fought to clear a way through the late-comers, like Moses parting the Red Sea. The organ sprang to life, the choir burst into tuneful hymns, and the performance was under way.

The congregation – those not seated – milled this way and that, chatting, pointing, coughing and hawking noisily, as Spaniards do, answering trilling mobile phones, some finally coming to the conclusion that they'd seen enough and going in search of a glass of orujo or a tumbler of Asturias' famous cider. Meanwhile, half a dozen well dressed grannies decided the pulpit was as good a place as any from which to view the proceedings.

The cathedral itself was started in the far off reign of Alfonso II, The Chaste, though it wasn't until the fourteenth century that it actually got going in any meaningful way. Almost three centuries later it was completed, so you can probably appreciate that it's quite a mélange of architectural styles, or 'distintos estilos', as the official brochure euphemistically puts it. But for all that, and the fact that its interior, at least, has the feeling of a big church, it seems all the better, all the more welcoming. And in its own way – and this is by no means faint praise – it's attractive and it has an atmosphere that other Spanish cathedrals – Zamora, Ciudad Rodrigo and Astorga, to name but three – decidedly lack. It's open and uncluttered from twin front doors to High Altar, and we liked it unreservedly. In addition, the Plaza de Alfonso II in front of the cathedral's façade gives the cathedral room to breathe and exhibit itself properly, as a good cathedral has every right to expect.

In this same square was a huge gantry and stage, at the farthest end, all readied for the evening's rock-cum-folk-cum-everything-else concert, and the square and the seemingly dozens of side-streets radiating from the square would be crammed to overflowing. There'd be singing and dancing and stalls of every kind and litter galore, and people of every age and shape, all noisy and good natured. They stare innocently at you out of curiosity, as is the Spanish way, and you stare back without malice in the certain knowledge that no offence will be taken. And you recall the number of times you've travelled by Merseyrail, head down and avoiding eye-contact. If you don't, you know you're inviting the remark of 'Who you lookin' at, shit-face?' Oh, to be in England, and I don't think so!

And it's like that all over this (in places) relatively modern city, not without its own history, you understand. This is the 'Muy Noble, muy Leal, Benemérita, Invicta, Heróica y Buena Ciudad de Oviedo' (and you won't need a dictionary for that, will you?). It thrived in medieval times under Alfonso II and Alfonso IV; it was never conquered by the marauding moors of North Africa; it rose against 'el invasor francés' in May, 1808; it boasts in its historic centre around the Flamboyant-Gothic cathedral, pre-Romanesque churches, and palaces and stately homes. And whilst what's known as the Commercial Centre of Oviedo dwarfs the medieval, historical centre, both seem to live comfortably cheek-to-cheek.

Here, it's 'relatively modern' thanks to the atrocities of the Spanish Civil War of 1936-1939 and Francisco Franco y Bahamonde, when the city, always a hot-bed of independent thought and well-organised workers' unions (dirty words in Franco's vocabulary) was bombed and bombarded. Franco had been here in 1934 to put down the miners' strikes in this most productive area of Spain (along with the Basque Provinces). He came at the behest of – wait for it! – the Socialist government of Theroux. Needless to say, but I will, Franco did his duty with unnecessary ferocity, killing people as if they were vermin.

So, after the Civil War, much of Oviedo was rebuilt, and splendidly so, with the wonderfully wide Calle Uría and equally impressive avenues at the heart of New Oviedo. There's the Auditorio Príncipe Felipe, a multi-purpose construction; the super-clean Plaza de América, the Paseo de los Álamos and Parque de San Francisco, the Casa Conde and the Teatro Campoamor.

And it's all so clean (unlike my Liverpool, I'm ashamed to say, on any morning of the week after another night of uncivilised behaviour. Have the English got something to learn about town planning and civilian cleanliness from Spanish cities! Have they indeed!).

So, it should come as no surprise to you that in 2007, the city of Oviedo, university city and cultural and commercial capital of the Principado de Asturias, was awarded The Golden Scrubbing Brush Award. And, by Jove, it's well merited, I can tell you. The day after the musical extravaganza in front of the cathedral, the whole square and surrounding streets were spotless by nine o'clock in the morning.

Go see if I'm right or not, and while you're at it, go and look at its graffiti-free street art all over the city, its statues and modern art, and smile at the sculpture of Woody Allen on the corner of Uría and Nacionales. Because that's what Oviedo did for two Hispanists and twenty-eight Australians who don't like big cities: it, and so many other things, made them smile.

17. Phythian, Moonie and Nicola Lyn

If you've taught Spanish at the top end of the secondary school level for thirty nine years – like what I have! – it's inevitable, I suppose, that some classes and groups and individuals will forever leave a mark on you, for better or worse (though I personally prefer to remember the best and dismiss the worst as an irrelevance: glass half full rather than half empty, that's my perception of things).

One such group of Advanced Level students was what I'll call The

Class of John Phythian, a group of ten pretty good lads and two constantly nervous girls in the very early 1990's.

They loved their Spanish, no doubt about it, though their collective inability to arrive remotely on time for their beloved Spanish class was slowly beginning to irritate me. In an unexpectedly diplomatic manner – completely out of character, I'll confess, and others will eagerly rush to agree with this view – I decided on a calmer approach in confronting the irritation.

It's Tuesday morning. At eleven o'clock on the dot, having had morning coffee in the fifteen minute break, I was back in the classroom on the top floor of the building before the bell sounded. It came as no great surprise to find that I was alone. I started the lesson, Gustavo Adolfo Bécquer's peerless poetry, as if all twelve were present.

Minutes later, they came noisily down the narrow passage way, past the Art Room and Brother Bownes' printing room, into the Spanish Room, Phythian's voice comfortably the loudest. Stopped suddenly when they realised something strange was going on, and created a domino effect and audible invective. Muttered voices and whispers, and they crawled in in dribs and drabs to find me speaking in Spanish to an empty classroom, writing on the blackboard to illustrate a particular point, and gesticulating, the better to get across my feelings about arguably Spain's greatest poet (and Stan Hayton and I will hear no argument about that, by the way).

The proverbial pin was dropped and distinctly heard, the double lesson went like a dream, Gustavo Adolfo was an unqualified success – not surprisingly – and not one of the twelve ever mentioned to me the incongruity of the moment. Nor did they ever again arrive late for Spanish. Well, not significantly late, that is.

About five years later, Nicola Lyn, out of the blue, phoned me one December day from Pontevedra – of all places! – and diplomatically reminded me about that Tuesday morning.

Nicola was not a beautiful girl by the warped standards of modern times, though she was certainly attractive in her own way. A naturally nervous girl, taciturn and reserved – who would possibly feel entirely at ease in Phythian's and Moonie's boisterously good natured company, I ask you! – Nicola was nevertheless a truly lovely person who worked doggedly and achieved beyond her abilities: my kind of student. Jonathan Mercer, lovely, lovely lad, was another. Still is.

"Nicola? Nicola Who? Oh, yes! Yes, yes, I remember you, of course I do! Nice of you to call! Where are you? Where? Pontevedra? Pontevedra in Galicia? That one? What on earth are you doing in Pontevedra, for goodness sake?"

Because she was a lovely girl – undoubtedly still is, thanks largely to her committed mother and her own natural qualities – she didn't take offence at my ill-disguised surprise that she had chosen Pontevedra as the place to do her year abroad. Pontevedra! A year! Jesus!

Of course, thirty-nine years teaching Spanish and fifty years visiting Spain made me an expert on all things Spanish, didn't it! No reply necessary, thank you very much, if it's all the same to you!

Now, that done, and sins publicly confessed, let's pause for a moment, shall we, and put Pontevedra into some sort of perspective, briefly comparing it to other Spanish towns and cities the length and breadth of the Peninsula.

It's far more attractive in every way than Benavente – what city wouldn't be, I hear you all knowledgably chorus – that city in Zamora province some seventy kilometres or so south of León, an eighty-kilometre stone's throw from Galicia's border. Whilst Benavente officially has four – yes, four! – monuments of interest in the entire city, the best by far, its castle-parador, is perched suitably high on a bluff, like all good castles should be. The only drawback is that it overlooks ugly cement factories and what's euphemistically called a business park which you can almost reach out and touch (and smell).

And Pontevedra's the proverbial streets ahead of distant, southerly Albacete, which boasts its Fábrica de Harinas – Flour Factory! – as one of its great attractions. That's the truth. So, enough said about distant Albacete, you'll say. Don't go there for the culture, then!

Badajoz is due west of infinitely superior Mérida in stunning Extremadura, hard up against Portugal's eastern border, but it's undeniably the poor relation of that exceptional western region of Spain. It's been the scene of so many wars over the last two thousand years that it's quite possibly the most shat-upon city in all Spain. So, Pontevedra comfortably bests Badajoz.

And it's ahead of the city of Palencia, too, in spite of its substantial number of churches and convents and monasteries (though few of them will leave you goggle-eyed and open-mouthed with admiration). And as for Verín, just inside Green Galicia's eastern border with Castilla-León, well, you really wouldn't want to be found dead there. Or alive, come to think of it! It's the one Spanish town where we've found absolutely nothing – nothing! – of merit.

On the other hand, let's be honest – Nicola! – Pontevedra is a million miles away from Toledo and Salamanca and Sevilla, but, then again, much the same can be said about almost any city, Spanish or otherwise.

So, having favourably compared Pontevedra to a few other Spanish cities, and briefly recognised its considerable limitations where yet others are concerned, what can we say about Pontevedra in its own right? What's it got to say about itself? And where is it, anyway?

Go and get your handy sized map of Spain, not too detailed, big enough to put on your knees, and we'll start from Madrid, shall we, since everyone knows where Madrid is – bang in the centre of the Iberian Peninsular, which is the main reason it was chosen as Spain's capital – and head for Tordesillas in a north-westerly direction.

On we go past Benavente – and going past Benavente is very possibly the best you can do, believe me – due west (or 'left', as Margaret technically says) along the A52, reluctantly bypassing charming Puebla de Sanabria, then featureless Verín, bash on in a north-westerly direction to sprawling Ourense, on along the rim of equally sprawling Vigo, and head due north. On a bad day and with the wind in an unfavourable direction you'll smell Pontevedra before you see it, thanks to the paper and dye factories along the Ría de Pontevedra.

In the 'old days' – pre 1995 according to Manuel: then again, 1995 is the 'old days' for him – Pontevedra was a chaotic place, full of drunks (he says) and ne'er-do-wells, suicidal traffic and pot-holed road surfaces, and few people wanted to live in the city. They even preferred Vigo (would you believe?), which should tell you how bad the situation was. Then, some fifteen years or so ago, Town Council and residents somehow got together with the decided intention of improving the whole city, 'to make a new atmosphere', as Manuel quaintly puts it.

Traffic, of course, is still something of a problem, though somehow things keep moving, and the explosion in the building of high rise flats (irrespective of parlous economic times) on seemingly every piece of vacant ground means Pontevedra can sometimes look like one big building site. And why, I frequently ask myself, build ever more flats when there's already more than enough to go around, when literally hundreds of them must surely be empty? Somebody has the answer: perhaps they could communicate it to me?

But, as a city with relatively little to commend it architecturally, it's nevertheless quite a nice place to walk and explore. The Monastery Church of San Francisco, with its single nave, is well worth a visit, as well as being a manifestly prayerful place, not always a characteristic of Spain's religious buildings.

Pontevedra's got no grand avenues (like Vigo, twenty kilometres away) but rather little back-streets of character, and hidden, unexpectedly pleasant squares and gardens and pedestrianised streets. Andrew – God rest his soul, which He surely will – sat happily under the arches and out of the November drizzle in the Praza de Verduras, quietly, contentedly drinking a couple of glasses of 'albariño', watching people and enjoying the peaceful moment. When we asked him what he wanted to do next he told us he'd like another 'albariño', please, and can we stay here a bit longer? And the Alameda in front of the Town Hall has been very much improved in every way: landscaped gardens, pruned trees, clean pathways. It's a credit to the authorities.

It's in the area of the 'Peregrina', with its recently re-decorated octagonal pilgrims' chapel, and the Church of San Francisco, hemmed in by Hacienda and over-looking Plaza de la Ferrería, that Pontevedra can be seen at its best. There's a nice feeling about the city as you people-watch or window-shop or slip into this or that bar or coffee house which Nicola must have fallen for (maybe fallen in and out of!) almost twenty years ago.

Living as we do, some twenty minutes outside the city in our mountain village, we're happy to go there every couple of weeks with Cael and his Mummy. Cael likes the bars and the coffee shops and Yves Rocher, even though he's only two and a half! Especially Yves Rocher.

Historically, legend has it that Greek traders might have come this far, and that Teucro, one of the heroes of the Trojan Wars, after being disowned by his father, founded Pontevedra, thereafter marrying Helen, daughter of Putrech. But since archaeological studies have shown no signs whatsoever of the existence of Pontevedra prior to Roman times, you have to wonder where the legend came from, since it's apparently totally without foundation. You wonder why it was ever mentioned in the first place! Still, who says tourist brochures have to be based on truth!

(Oh, and whilst I'm on the subject of tourist brochures and associated matters: even if English is your first language, don't, whatever you do, go to (almost) any tourist office in Spain and ask for tourist information about their city in English. They've been translated literally from the original Spanish, dictionary in one hand, brainless biro in the other, into utterly nonsensical English by some bugger who hasn't got a clue but collects a substantial amount of money for the task. Isn't it time the authorities got a grip? The number of times I've seen English-speaking tourists laughing hysterically, eyes weeping, holding themselves barely upright against some lamp post or shop window in an effort to contain themselves, fanning themselves with their English translation of a Spanish information leaflet, crying hysterically that "I'm going to wet meself in a minute!" Funny it might be, acceptable it certainly isn't. It's the same with a significant number of those purporting to be English speaking tour guides: saying 'they haven't got a clue' is being nice to them, believe me. Now, don't get me going on about that one in Burgos, whatever you do!)

Anyway, let's get back to history – verifiable history, that is, which is not always Spain's forte – and accept that the Romans did indeed get this far and named the place Pons Vecchius, which eventually became the (translated) name we know it by today.

Once upon a time – throughout the Middle Ages and up to the sixteenth century – Pontevedra was considered one of the principal ports of Galicia. Columbus' 'Santa María' was built here. Thereafter, and for entirely political reasons, the city was largely abandoned by the crown of Castilla, and there followed numerous wars, none of them to Pontevedra's advantage.

To add insult to injury, the River Lérez flowing through the city silted up and Pontevedra's status as a port of consequence passed to geographically better placed Vigo, with the result that the 'Ría' (inlet) is now mainly for recreational use (when it's not being used as a receptacle of largely untreated industrial waste).

All along the beautiful coast of Galicia, from Vigo and Pontevedra and beyond Finisterre and the Costa da Mort, the 'rías' are natural indentations. And though the 'Ría de Pontevedra' may have suffered less than others, it nevertheless felt the catastrophe caused by the 'Prestige'.

On 19 November, 2002, in the foulest of foul weathers, this Liberian single hull tanker, constructed (badly) in Japan in 1976, and now under the flag of convenience of Bahamas, carrying 77,000 tons of 'fuel', eventually split in two and went down in a Force Eight gale and six metre waves some two hundred and fifty kilometres west of Finisterre. By the by, its lack of sea worthiness had twice been penalised in 1991 with heavy fines.

Six days earlier, on 13 November, the tanker had its first experience of the storm and edged out towards the South Atlantic in the hope of finding marginally calmer waters and off-loading its filthy cargo. It was already listing at a forty-five degrees angle and leaking badly. Three days later, the first oil reached the Galician coast, but Aznar's government declared it nothing more than 'manchas localizadas', belatedly confessing that 'la situación no es nada buena'. But Nature would take care of itself! Just you wait and see! Ha!

Manuel Fraga Iribarne – and let's name names, shall we – ex-Franco henchman and great survivor of Franco days and the then President of Galicia, took eight (eight!) days to witness the catastrophe for himself: he was on holiday, after all, and couldn't be arsed. And José María Aznar – the Ronnie Corbett look-alike and soon to be deposed Prime Minister, all smarmy and distant with a moustache of no significance – waited thirty-one

137

days (not a misprint) before visiting Galicia. Even then, he didn't go near the worst affected areas, nor did he appear in the nation's Parliament, leaving poor, listless, charisma-less Rajoy as the government's under-briefed spokesman.

Not merely that, either. After dithering whether or not it was best to bomb the 'Prestige' to the bottom of the Atlantic, tow it to some port or another in a Force Eight gale, or siphon off its filth to other vessels (again, I remind you, in a Force Eight gale and six metre waves), Aznar did nothing.

I tell a lie! He instructed the Spanish press – and this is verifiably true, by the way – that he'd withhold any (belated) help to the thousands of Galicians affected if reporters exposed the naked truth of the matter. He was roundly and justifiably denounced by the Colegio de Peridodistas de Galicia for his embargo on flights over the stricken area to record the catastrophe, though, in all probability, that didn't bother Aznar. Happily, though not for Galicians, Ronnie Corbett's spineless double fell from power two years later. Unhappily for Galicians – and the rest of Spain, if it comes to that – Aznar, like that other chameleon, Blair, has reinvented himself as a moderate and a player on the world's wider (unelected) political stage, where he can say things and not have to answer to anyone.

Since he managed to lose the 2004 election, in spite of having a more than comfortable 7% lead in the polls, and having stupidly blamed ETA for the Madrid bombings of that year which killed one hundred and ninety-one people, even after it became obvious to any idiot that ETA had nothing to do with it, Aznar somehow managed to convince a significant number of people that he was whiter than snow in everything. He's currently making a proverbial mint in USA giving lectures on political leadership; at the time of writing, he's on the board of News International; and in 2010 he was appointed to chair the Advisory Council of the Global Adaptation Institute, a body which concerns itself with adaptation to climate change.

Is it any surprise that Spaniards in general – and, for our present purposes, Galicians in particular – revile José María Aznar, all-round goody-goody, able to rise from the shit of his own making, smelling like a rose?

But make no mistake: God is good and Aznar will get his come uppance, believe me! And Blair, too! Oh, please God, Blair, too! Blair, most especially! And the despicable Mandelson.

And you'll surely want to know this, too, to put the whole sorry mess into some sort of context.

In the prologue of a book published by FAES in 2011 called 'El Ecologismo Sensato en España', written by Verónica Lipperheide, Azaña writes that an 'ecologista sensato' is exactly the definition of his own political stance with regards to the environment. He goes on to say that he was a pioneer in the defence of nature conservation, and that his was the first (and only) government in Spanish history to create the post of Minister for the Environment. 'Correct on this last point, mendacious bastard on the rest', is what Galicians would call him, with utter conviction and justification.

But Pontevedra's 'ría' did suffer (even if 'less than others'). Its sandy beaches and innumerable rocky inlets were randomly covered with the copious filth – the 'chapapote' – and the livelihood of its numerous fishermen (and those in the countless related industries) was severely affected. In the short term, all its marine life was destroyed, to recover only slowly in subsequent years.

There was born a movement of 'voluntarios' from all over Spain, not just Galicia, who worked with shovels and spades and bare hands – it's 2002, folks! – in an effort to clear up the coastline; and the slogan, 'Nunca Máis!' ('Never Again!') was a rallying cry which was to haunt and taunt gutless politicians after the environmental catastrophe of the 'Prestige':

though, of course Fraga and Rajoy are still around, in spite of proven incompetence.

Oh, and just in case you have the slightest sympathy for slimey Aznar, let me remind you that in 1992 the 'Mar Egeo' went down in the same area with a slightly less catastrophic result, and the government of the day acted – if such is the correct verb to use – in similar fashion. You have to come to the independently reached conclusion that Galicia, yet again, is of another galaxy where Madrid is concerned. That's certainly the feeling in Galicia, and who can gainsay them? Little wonder they look down their noses at Madrid, and insist on the continued existence of their own 'gallego' language.

You might want to know this, too.

After the 'Prestige' disaster, an embarrassed government correctly thought it owed the people of Galicia a thing or two, so it made several promises. Three or four more paradors would be built in Galicia to improve the local economy. Almost ten years later, they have yet to open their doors, nor will they in the foreseeable future.

Galicians were also promised that the AVE (Tren de Alta Velocidad) would join up Galicia with the rest of Spain, and in particular Madrid, and a very considerable amount of money has been lavished on that apparently worthy project. It won't be ready for a number of years yet, largely because the topography of this part of Spain is an enormous challenge; but the question has to be asked: how on earth can such a venture possibly benefit Galicia, when few Galicians will want or need to travel to Madrid anyway, when Galicia's got three airports, all new, when Ryanair puts on three ridiculously cheap flights every day from Santiago de Compostela, to say nothing of Air Europa and Spanair? Galicians, in spite of their long history of necessary emigration to the Americas and all over Europe in search of work, are arguably, amongst Spaniards, the most wedded to their region.

Everybody knows that, even politicians without a brain, and there seem to be a superfluity of them. Which begs a further question: what have Galician politicians done for Galicia other than allowing their fellow 'gallegos' to have the shit kicked out of them by the central government in Madrid? Please, somebody enlighten me.

And matters have worsened, since the internal rail infrastructure – in the shape of the fundamental need for the much more important 'trenes de cercanías' – has been downgraded, with the result that there are fewer local trains for 'gallegos' to use. Bloody soft or what? An important place like Arcade, in the south of the province, will have its stopping-trains drastically reduced. Thanks a bundle, Aznar and a host of insignificant others: snouts back into the trough, then, lads.

But, for all that, Pontevedra's not finished yet, not by a very long chalk. The streets are clean, the people well dressed and good natured and tacitly sure that better times are coming; the coffee houses are full, and Zara and Punt Roma do good business, even in these difficult times. Go into Pontevedra on any day of the week, and most especially before lunch, and the shops are crowded and people are buying, and no self-respecting denizen will go without his daily coffee and a cake. Add to this the relative but growing importance of the city as part of the Camino Portugués on its way northwards to Santiago de Compostela, together with a significant 'third age' tourism slowly starting to make its mark, and it's hard not to feel some cautious optimism where Pontevedra is concerned. And if and when this happens, it will be no credit to the politicians, either: let's be clear on that point. If Nicola came back today, she could only agree, and be proud of 'her' Pontevedra.

Post script.

I went to Pontevedra railway station the other day to pick up a timetable for future reference. Crossing the road, I was delighted to see a car with an English registration in the car park. The passenger in the front seat was trying to feed the parking ticket through her window into the machine which would raise the barrier and let them out. It wasn't happening for them, so I went over to see if I might help.

"Good morning! Having a problem?"

"The bloody machine isn't working."

"Have you tried feeding the ticket in with the arrow pointing up?"

"Course I bloody have. Just told you, it doesn't bloody work. Press that 'i' button there. Maybe that'll open it."

Nothing deterred by the distinct lack of friendliness and only mildly miffed at the clear lack of basic manners to a fellow countryman (now more than happily living in Galicia, and thankfully no longer a fellow countryman), I did what the increasingly frustrated driver suggested.

Over the crackling intercom I was told in Spanish to go to the payment booth about thirty yards away. I translated this for the three occupants.

"What? You're telling me we actually have to pay here? You're telling me it's not free? It says 'libre' on that sign there, doesn't it? That means 'free', doesn't it?"

"Ah, yes, but all that means is that there's actually spaces available. It doesn't mean you don't have to pay. Will you be able to make yourself understood in the payment booth, or can I help?"

"Course I bloody will. They'll understand English, won't they?"

Arse-holes.

18. Quiroga

I've tried with singular diligence – even if I do say so myself – to give you good value, Reader, in terms of travel in Spain via the twenty-seven letters of the Spanish alphabet. Believe me when I tell you that there have been times I would gladly have left out one or two: K and W come quickly to mind, and Mieres isn't far behind them, either, though that's probably a reflection on the place, rather than the letter M. (Nevertheless, even Mieres has a place in the fond-memory section simply because of the then youngsters Paul and I were with in August 1970. You don't forget them in a hurry, I'm telling you.)

Alternatively, some have been easy and have tripped off the word-processor (or the pencil, in my particular case, since everything's written in long-hand in the first instance, on any paper that comes to hand). Almagro and Salamanca and Toledo are just such examples, and I think the enthusiasm shows through (even if I do say so myself).

But along with the aforementioned K and W, the letter Q was not an easy one, in spite of the fact that, on the surface, at least, there are more than one hundred and fifty possibilities. Yet, consider this: of the initially encouraging number to play with, there are twenty-seven tiny settlements called Quintana Something-or-Other (Quintana del Monte, Quintana del Pino, Quintana-María, as random examples); and there's a whopping fifty-one equally tiny settlements called Quintanilla Something-or-Other (Quintanilla de Arriba, Quintanilla de Onésimo, Quintanilla de Urz, along with forty-eight other Quintanillas).

By far the vast majority of this aggregate of nearly eighty places share either one or more of the following characteristics with the remaining (unnamed) seventy or so: nobody but their own inhabitants has ever heard of them; they are so insignificant that on some road maps they fail to gain a mention; there are more dilapidated or totally ruined houses ('hovels' might be a better word) than inhabited dwellings; they're on the road from Nowhere to Nowhere; they have minimal impact, at very best, on anything remotely associated with the word 'interest'; few, if any of them, are of even the slightest importance in the great scheme of things, though the odd miffed denizen might feel obliged to fight his corner, if only out of misplaced pride and loyalty.

Quiroga is a case in point.

We two were on the way to spend a few nights in Villafranca del

Bierzo (which has come to rival Reinosa and Toro and Puebla de Sanabria for an elevated place in our lasting affections). We'd been impressed by the scenery in parts of the province of Lugo, and everywhere that the Valley of the Sil meanders through Ourense Province: high peaks covered in December mists and cloud; valleys way down below the level of the N 120, as it twists this way and that, climbing and falling on its way past Monforte de Lemos and San Clodio on its way towards Villafranca, our destination; and the Sil, alternately wide and narrow, peaceful and cascading, stopped here and there by ugly hydro-electric plants. And since the N120 passes along the edge of Quiroga, and since, with its almost four thousand inhabitants, Quiroga starts with the letter Q, with an open mind and our usual boundless enthusiasm and optimism we took the opportunity offered.

Let's stop to establish verifiable facts which, by their very nature, are independent of opinions and bias.

Quiroga exists to some extent on agriculture, the raising and the pasturing of cattle, a certain amount of mining, and is rightly proud of its unique place and involvement in the production of the more than acceptable Ribeira Sacra wines. In fact, during Holy Week, it has hosted its own Wine Fair for the last (almost) thirty years.

And, in a part of Spain where you would certainly not expect to see them, given the climate and the soil, neither of them very hospitable, it's the biggest olive producer outside of Andalucía and Extremadura. Now, there's a thing! It has to be hastily added, however, that this is no big deal, as they say, since olives are the inalienable prerogative of these huge, largely under-populated areas, and Quiroga's role really is marginal in the very extreme.

But it's the good old 'service industries' which are the town's biggest employers by far, which doesn't say a lot for the employment possibilities in the region. Service industries, by their very nature, are the comparative realm of the few, and those few are, in the main, the better educated or those with better contacts, which must leave a very significant percentage of the population of Quiroga and other settlements beyond the pail. And, frankly, we were less than remotely impressed by those we came into contact with on that Saturday in the very early days of December, 2011.

We parked on what seemed to be the main street of what seemed to be the quintessential one-horse-town. I'd give you the name of the street, but having walked it more than once from one dreary end to the other, we failed to find a plaque giving such vital, if elementary, information. Nevertheless, nothing deterred and being hungry, we popped into bar after cafetería after restaurant in search of basic sustenance. The compound adjective 'fly-blown' comes instantly to mind. We walked back streets and side streets and its nameless main street, looked through windows and opened doors to identity what was on offer, and we found nothing to fulfil minimal demands.

They were full, which seems to suggest that some people were satisfied, if satisfaction consists of wall-to-wall noise in the form of loud conversation, supplemented by a monster television at full belt in the corner, nobody listening; 'Deliverance' type looks from suddenly silent drinkers when we opened the door; a mixture of the sumptuously well-dressed and the badly-dressed and – in the case of a significant number of the female population on show – the hardly dressed, all floppy and falling about; and an off-putting odour of badly prepared food, long on unprotected show on the bar counter, and an unseen toilet somewhere beyond the back wall.

The décor, if such is the word, was less than impressive. It might well have been all-the-rage back in the 1950s in this neck of the woods, but it did absolutely nothing for us. We grabbed a hasty coffee, which brought a tear to our eyes, and an even hastier 'empanada', made with what seemed like leather instead of a gentle pastry covering, located the car, shook the dust from our shoes, and beat an equally hasty retreat, finding the road to Villafranca del Bierzo in something approaching record time. We looked at each other in that wordless way which is worth a thousand words, and burst into laughter.

Of course, the distinct possibility is that we caught Quiroga on a less than good day; our expectations may have been ridiculously high; our demands may well have been unreasonable. But I do recall, with immediate and consummate ease, a telling phrase used by Our Dennis (who has a way with words, let me tell you): a kiss-me-arse place. It's hard to argue with this conclusion where Quiroga is concerned.

The positive side, however, is that I've managed to write marginally more than twelve hundred words on a settlement starting with the letter Q, which, while it's unlikely to merit much time and effort, may have given you some gentle entertainment, Reader.

19. I can't remember

I can't remember the name of the hotel we were thrown out of sometime before breakfast in mid August 1970. We decided, Paul and I, that in the circumstances it might not be the most sensitive thing to do to stay for breakfast, even if it was included in the price for the rooms.

I do seem to recall somewhat distantly and indistinctly that it was in a small, fairly modest square no great distance from the centre of Ribadesella, but, to be honest with you, Reader, I'm not sure I'd be able to find it again, forty years later, except, perhaps, by complete accident. I remember that it was quite nice – at least it was as far as two adults and ten teenagers were concerned (and before the 'incident') – rooms only (with breakfast in the hotel's bar on street level), three floors, no lift, about thirty rooms in all, and you could see the beach from some of the rooms.

After Ávila (where John Burke had played cricket under the walls with a rolled newspaper for a bat, to the consternation of the natives) and León, and the aberration that was Mieres, we'd driven in a generally northerly direction in what seemed like total silence after the late night and the alcohol fuelled karaoke in funereal Mieres. We'd been on the road for almost two weeks (with a rest of four days or so in Madrid's steaming capital city: Hostal Fuencarral, Calle Fuencarral, just off Gran Vía), and we'd got to know each others' foibles and eccentricities more in that short time than in the four years we'd spent in a classroom together in Saint Francis Xavier's College, Woolton, Liverpool 25. But we were all still talking to each other, still chums: never a cross word without an apology. I do remember that. That was nice.

I can't think we headed for Ronnie's Gijón because I don't remember any big city on our way; but I do remember mountains. Lots and lots of mountains, nasty looking and wildly abrupt and not meant for climbing, except, I suppose, by people who like climbing nasty looking, wildly abrupt mountains. And there were winding roads through lunar landscapes, and hot sun through a bug-speckled windscreen. Ten drowsy lads behind me, some sleeping, others in companionable silence, Kenny Vaughan's round, mischievous face (and severe fringe) always alert and watching me and Paul and the scenery.

We stopped a few times for the usual necessities: stretch the legs, find a toilet (or anywhere you could do your toilet in relative peace and privacy), have a drink and a bite to eat, climb a hill and slither down the slate slopes. We must have turned off somewhere near Pola de Siero, across country and generally parallel with the distant coastal road (no distance on the map, hours away in reality, then and even now). Maybe we stopped at or went through Cangas de Onís or Arriondas. I've no clear idea, since long ago – by which I mean as soon as we'd left Liverpool! – I'd delegated the minutiae of the daily route to Paul, and I can't remember ever having regretted that unspoken accord.

What I do remember with certainty is the reason for making Ribadesella our stop for that night. The Lads between them had been delegated the task of generally loading and unloading and keeping (relatively) tidy the interior of the orange Ford Transit, and it was rumoured that Stephen Lennon 'knew a bit about engines and cars' (based on the flimsy fact that it was generally accepted that he intended to do Physics at A Level and his headmaster-father had a car! And Stephen had a lovely sister!).

So, when steam started to blow back onto the windscreen from beneath the bonnet not long after we left Mieres, it became clear to the least scientific amongst us (to wit, the driver) that we had a problem. We stopped at a petrol station on the edge of Ribadesella and left the Transit there overnight.

Let's tarry a while whilst you go and get yourself a basic, handy sized map of Spain (again). First, find Madrid, bang in the centre. Go north in the straightest of straight lines until you get to the sea. That's Santander. Look west – or left, as Margaret would technically have it – and find Oviedo (not on the coast, but only marginally inland). Almost midway between Santander and Oviedo, on the coast road, you'll find Ribadesella (or Ribeseya, in the Asturian dialect).

Its name means 'on the banks of the River Sella' (which is, indeed, where it's located). It's got around six thousand inhabitants, and since, with its lovely beaches, it's something of a summer magnet for Spanish tourists, that figure can comfortably double throughout July and August, much to the delight of the town's hotels and business community. Accommodation during that time cannot be assured for love nor money unless you reserve your room months in advance (which we hadn't done, but, then again, it was forty years ago, and Spaniards weren't the wealthiest of Europeans, and foreign tourists in this neck of the woods – and even today – were few and far between).

Nowadays, there's a proliferation of hotels – about four dozen – which do good summer business, in spite of 'la crisis' to which Zapatero seems to have conveniently turned a blind eye. (The Spanish equivalent, by the way is 'to make a fat view'. Thought you'd like to know. Another little gem for Quiz Night.)

And, since Ribadesella's coastal with a benign climate and fresh air blowing in off the Bay of Biscay, there's been an explosion of campsites, all of which are easily as good as, and frequently better than, anywhere else in Europe. There's lots of noise, of course, it being Spain.

It was founded in the mid thirteenth century – Ribadesella, not the campsite, you understand – by Alfonso X, more frequently known as Alfonso El Sabio (The Wise), who boasts an enviable curriculum: poet of considerable distinction, though Alf, Castilian to the very marrow, wrote his celebrated 'cantigas' in Galician Spanish; a man of personal and widely admired scholarship, during whose reign he encouraged scholarship in everything from astrology to chess to literature to music and much beyond; a political reformer and unifier; a staunch supporter of the pre-eminence of Castilian Spanish (in spite of the 'cantigas'). In fact, pretty much a Renaissance Man long before the appearance of the Renaissance.

I digress – marginally – but I bet you got some pleasure from knowing about Alfonso, didn't you! Quite a lad, you'll agree. There have been thirteen Alfonsos on the Spanish throne, too, the last one booted out in 1931 to live in comfortable exile, thereby missing out on the Spanish Civil War. Some more utterly enthralling facts for the Pub Quiz.

Now, I hear you say, let's get back to the ten lads and their two teachers, shall we, and kindly stop rambling. Will do!

If Ribadesella were not on the coast, it would in all probability be just another fairly insignificant spot on the map. But for ten young lads who had spent the previous two weeks and more in the arid interior of what was then called Castilla La Vieja – Old Castile – far from anything remotely like water, the wide, bow-like, beautiful beach of Playa de Santa Marina was a blessing. They went loopy and childlike, trying to drown each other or bury chums up to their eyes in the fine sand; built sand castles and kicked them down; admired Spanish beauties with their tongues out and their eyes on stilts; had a great time doing exactly what any sixteen year old should do.

And since they were all from Liverpool, where football and music were currently king, they clubbed together and bought a ball and we had a six-a-side game on the wide stretches of the beach, the touch lines being the tide and the sea wall. Of course, some were better athletes than others, some greater devotees of the game than others, and as a nation with a long memory we were still basking in the glorious (if fortuitous) World Cup win over The Huns, four years previously.

John McAlinden, a willowy youth who walked more on his toes than the soles of his feet, and for whom football was a tad too rough, had to be frequently reminded that "We're playin' footy over 'ere, you know, McAlinden!" when John strayed once too often to the pools left by the outgoing tide which he used as a mirror to comb his top heavy Elvis Presley quiff. To this simple kick-about, Kenny brought the same degree of endeavour and conviction always in evidence on Saturday morning interschool games, so he couldn't understand John's less than fulsome interest and lack of commitment.

Paul, whose forte lay more in intense involvement than any natural finesse where football was concerned, proceeded to tackle anything and everything that moved, though not at all in any malicious way, you understand. Once launched, he found it difficult to pull back. One of his tackles on that sun drenched afternoon left its size twelve impression (and fourteen stones in body weight) on all parts of my left foot, with the result that by next morning it was discoloured and bloated and immensely painful when changing gears on the Transit's tank-like clutch pedal. Ever the consummate actor, I hammed it up, though I really was incapacitated. Passing Spaniards watched the whole event with great interest, and wondered how the Invincible Armada could possibly have been defeated by our ancestors.

We knew that on the following morning the GCE results would be published in far away Saint Francis Xavier's College, Woolton, Liverpool 25, so we unanimously decided that Mass on the following morning after breakfast might make all the difference in the world. They were the days, of course, when public examinations actually did examine hard work and preparation and ability rather than the apology they've subsequently become over the last twenty years.

I'm sure we must have dined well that night. Paul and I promised to give them all a wake-up call next morning. As we went up the stairs from our floor to theirs just before nine o'clock, we wondered why the hotel staff had washed down the stone steps at this early hour, instead of waiting for guests to leave later that morning. On the boys' landing, it was wetter still. It was too wet to be natural. We looked at each other.

We knocked on the first door, opened it, and a carpet floated by, along the landing, draping itself over the steps on its downward path.

Kenny and John Burke were sitting on their beds in their football shorts – sky blue – their feet lifted in the air, a distant look of incomprehension on their faces, their suitcases moving gently of their own volition. Meanwhile, the wash basin continued to overflow. To judge by the amount of water, this must have started some time previously, and with the not unexpected results in other parts of the hotel.

One of them had been sick in the night, it transpires, and for some unexplained reason – which we didn't immediately pursue, given the gravity of the moment: still don't know to this day, though we suspect! – couldn't locate the toilet. So the wash basin, conveniently on hand, was used, became blocked, and the tap had 'somehow' been left on.

We left the hotel in what must have been a new world record. Paul kindly offered to go down and pay the bill and face the manager's justified wrath, which was not placated by the few hundred pesetas left to assist with the drying out of the hotel. Paul said the manager used a lot of words he'd never known existed in Spanish, but he got the poor man's general drift.

I do recall quite clearly the absence of goodwill evidenced by two teachers towards ten teenage students. I don't recall when something approaching normal relationships were resumed, though it might well have been when we picked up Stephen Moore's case on the return visit to Angouleme, where Paul arranged a sumptuous meal in a fairly dingy French restaurant, possibly a turning point, and enjoyed by one and all.

You may be surprised to be told that not one of the visitors to that Ribadesella hotel in August 1970 has ever been back to this pleasant seaside town in Asturias in the intervening forty years. Margaret and I passed through about ten years ago but decided not to tarry.

154

20. Lorenzo's Salamanca

In the late, glorious summer of 1965, Ellen-Mae Gotobed, Birmingham Mick, her intended, and I eventually left Coimbra after three months of paying lip-service to a course in Portuguese language, literature and history, organised and sponsored by the Nubar Gulbenkian Foundation. We were bound for Madrid. In spite of the down-at-heel nature of almost everything in Portugal's premier university city, and our own inability (not that we tried very hard, I have to say) to master a language which manages to sound like nasal Russian, we'd somehow loved every minute of our time there; loved each other's companionship (loved even Andrew, majoring for a PhD in Misery); loved the days spent in Atlantic Figueira da Foz (when we should, by rights, have been attending some lecture or other); loved Aveiro and Batalha and Alcobaça and Leiria; loved everything, even the monotony of cod and spaghetti and cod and spaghetti and cod.

But Madrid was to see our parting of the ways. They'd go off to a similarly soon-to-be-ignored course in Barcelona, me to the University of Sevilla, where three months of alcoholic intemperance would finally catch up with me: not a boast, but rather a belated confession. Mea culpa, mea culpa, mea maxima culpa. We thought we would live forever.

First, though, we decided to get off the slowly-moving Madrid-bound train and spend a few days in Salamanca, my first-ever visit, and it's there that we were arrested by the Guardia Civil. Well, I was.

The train got into Salamanca just after midnight, dawdling from Coimbra in an easterly direction, so we three decided to get a taxi into the city centre, no great distance away, but we were disinclined to lug our cases any distance at all. Mick knew a place, he said, where all three of us could put up in one room for a few nights, cutting down the cost by sharing.

A taxi pulled away from the rank, the driver shouting at us from the open window that he'd be back for us in ten minutes or so. We nodded. Another taxi came along fifteen minutes later, so we hopped in. When we got to our destination – I've no memory at all of where it dropped us off: none at all – the first taxi, which had been frantically following us, cut in front of us and demanded payment for the promise he said we'd made him. Mick told him to go away with jerking movements, and manually interpreted this advice in a clearer fashion, just in case the enraged taxi driver had failed to understand the spoken word. Mick was very good with people, and I liked his style.

We three went straight to our beds in a small room in some unnamed guest house down some unnamed side street, probably just outside the cultural nucleus of classy Salamanca. Around four o'clock that morning, there was an angry hammering on our door. Mick eventually got up to investigate, came back to say the police – two Civil Guards – wanted to see all three of us outside.

Do bear in mind that this was only twenty-five brief years after the Spanish Civil War had ended, and that Franco and his fellow reprobates were very much in charge of very much everything. And an unexplained, unexpected visit in the early hours of the morning by the still-feared Guardia Civil was no laughing matter, señor.

One of them took my arm in a manner which left no room for doubt, shook me menacingly, and advised me that I was under arrest. Why me, Lord? Mick, who towered over them, and whose Spanish was streets ahead of mine, explained the truth of the matter to their eventual satisfaction. They then turned their baleful, intimidating eyes to the taxi driver, whom we were happy to leave to his fate.

But, that cameo apart, where on earth do you start with Salamanca? What can you possibly say about it that's not been said before, this Spanish-Oxford which comfortably surpasses English Oxford at every level, this city of 160,000 inhabitants, the second largest, after cheerless Valladolid, in that huge wedge called Castilla-León, just over two-hundred kilometres west of Madrid?

Thirty years after this minor incident, Gerard (whom I'd been privileged to meet for the first time in the first week of September, 1966, in a French lesson in 2A classroom in Saint Francis Xavier's College, Woolton, Liverpool 25) whole-heartedly agreed to come with me on a Spanish adventure which was to be the celebration of a 'significant' birthday. This, of course, was before he met Ann! Our only plan was to get to Madrid and, entirely at my suggestion, to make our way westwards to Extremaduran Cáceres. Being the gentleman he is and always has been, he did not question my judgement.

We stayed three days in Madrid's broiling summer heat, visiting the sights, as you do, and going off to Toledo and Segovia and Ávila, where The Class of '66, Gerard included, had stayed in 1970. After three superb days in simply superb Salamanca, we headed out by bus to Cáceres, in Gerard's case with just the slightest glimpse of reluctance. At the end of what seemed endless hours in ninety degrees of heat in a bus with no air conditioning, sweating like pigs and out of sorts, we got off in Cáceres' dust-blown, summer-over-heated bus station, got a basic room (shower, toilet, both down the hall) above an all-night pharmacy, washed and went out to take a look around.

Now, it's a statement of fact that Cáceres is a jewel of Extremadura, that land-locked, achingly beautiful, traditionally impoverished area along Portugal's eastern border. Its old town is a glorious living monument to a glorious past, its modern city not bad at all, as modern cities go, even if we found a less obvious welcome there than in other parts of Spain. Nevertheless, it's spoken of with admiration and awe by those who would sorely like to visit it: a place you simply must go and see before you hand in your pail. Cuca, up there is distant Reinosa, always spoke of it with the utmost respect and awe, promising herself she would go there to live. Of course, it wasn't to be.

If I tell you that Gerard's first words were: "You honestly mean to tell me we left Salamanca for this?" If I tell you that he couldn't get out of Cáceres fast enough – we left the next afternoon for Salamanca, and he was delirious with happiness! – it might just tell you something about the lure of Salamanca.

So, going back to the semi-rhetorical question set some five paragraphs ago (sorry about the diversion; I tend to get excited when I remember Salamanca): "where on earth do you start with Salamanca"?

It might be a bit glib and simplistic to suggest that the main square of any village or town or city in Spain is the best place; but when you're talking about Salamanca, it's hard to suggest a better location to begin, undoubtedly the very finest in all Spain (and no other opinion will be tolerated!).

Put simply, it's an absolute stunner. It was designed by the celebrated Churriguera brothers – What do you mean, you've never heard of them! Come on! – and it took twenty-five brief years to complete. It was actually commissioned by Philip V for the citizens of Salamanca, who supported his cause in the eighteenth century War of Spanish Succession. If there's one single and singular place of reference and meeting point, it's surely got to be here.

Under porticoes on all four sides, and spilling over a good half dozen metres into the square in the hot Castilian summer, there's tables and chairs full of locals and visitors and Americans – they adore Salamanca, so there can't be that much wrong with Americans, comparatively speaking – chatting and drinking and nibbling and people-watching right up until midnight and beyond. And when the light eventually fails as the sun goes down, you see the square lit up in its evening attire. From the half dozen or more streets radiating from the square, still they come, the locals and the visitors and the Americans.

The problem with Salamanca, if, indeed, you consider it to be a problem, is where to go next, because this oldest university-city par excellence, replete with the very best in Renaissance and Plateresque architecture; this former (and, surely, continuing) European Capital of Culture for 2002; this tourist city, largely unaffected by the huge and continuing influx of tourists: it's the tourists that change, not the city; this former wasteland – yes, it was, believe it or not! – for almost four hundred years after the Moors conquered it in 712, thereafter undisputedly one of Spain's greatest monuments to its past … has so very much to offer, in spite of the fact that the French, of course, were here around 1808, and they all but destroyed it, of course.

Left and right, behind and in front of you, there's museums and churches and chapels and convents and palaces and university book shops by the veritable score (and there's some fantastic bars and restaurants, to boot).

So let's make our leisurely way out of the square and down the Rúa Mayor, with its bars and restaurants and necessary gift shops to left and right, all against a background of good-humoured crowds and the obligatory Spanish insistence on noise, until it opens out; and there before us are Salamanca's cathedrals: 'cathedrals' plural because, like my Liverpool, though infinitely greater, the city fathers of long ago were somehow not satisfied with the Old Cathedral, though only God Himself can explain why.

It was built in the twelfth and thirteenth centuries and its (basically) single nave gives it all the warmth and intimacy of a church, rather than the hyperbole that cathedrals are sometimes wont to favour. It's small, compact, welcoming, prayerful and immensely appealing, whilst its 'retablo' (altar piece), from floor to ceiling, is astonishing in its beauty and intricacy. So, and I consciously repeat myself for effect, only God Himself can explain why a new cathedral was deemed necessary.

It was started in 1513 and was eventually consecrated in its final form almost two hundred and fifty years later, and, in its own right, it, too, is an absolute stunner (though not, of course, in everybody's view when comparisons with the Old Cathedral are made). And as a result of the two and a half centuries it took to complete, it's a mixture of Gothic, Late

Gothic, Renaissance and Baroque styles (and probably lacks, shall we say, a certain uniformity, but it certainly stops you and makes you look at least twice). Tellingly, perhaps, the city's fathers wanted the New Cathedral to have some connection with the Old Cathedral, so both religious monuments share one wall, which is something of a novelty.

Meanwhile, in 1755, some four hundred kilometres to the south-east of Salamanca, the force of the Lisbon Earthquake was such that both cathedrals suffered structural damage, and to this day inspections and ongoing work can be seen. It must have been one bugger of a bang, when you come to think of it, to have caused the damage.

If you go a dozen or so metres down the gently sloping street, you can actually see the River Tormes from here with its Roman Bridge, built in the first century A.D., and retaining fifteen of its original twenty-six arches. It was here that Lazarillo's blind master – an absolute bastard, but who also taught the orphaned lad a thing or two about life at the sharp end of the social scale – came a cropper when Lázaro had him jump a non-existent puddle, thereby smashing his head against a strategically placed stone lion.

And if you want to walk down the street to the river – which we won't on this occasion, if it's all the same to you: we're pushed for time as it is, and there's so much more you'll want to see – you can look back and up towards this super city and get the most beautiful panoramic view imaginable.

And, perhaps on another occasion, you might want to stop at the relatively recently inaugurated Civil War Museum. I guarantee that you'll be suitably chastened by what you see and learn about that terrible conflict, largely unknown to non-Spaniards, and now officially consigned to history, but still a vital aspect of those, now elderly, whose lives were so signally affected by it.

Anyway, let's cross the pedestrianised street in front of both cathedrals and see who this fellow on a plinth is. Why, it's Don Miguel de Unamuno, born a Basque (which we won't hold against him), and once, for forty-six years, Professor of Greek at the university. A philosopher of some standing, never at a loss for words and always in search of an audience for his ideas, he was also a poet and a novelist; and for our pains, Stan and I waded through his stodgy, turgid offerings with little enthusiasm in Liverpool University's Victoria Building, top floor, cavernous and draughty lecture rooms, in The Truly Wonderful Sixties. We knew him as 'Una-bloody-Muno', when we felt charitable. He had other names when we couldn't work out what he was trying to say, and wondered why we were even reading him when there were so many other more profitable things we might be doing.

We also had to study the poetry of Fray Luis de León, whose statue is just around the corner and, entirely fittingly, in front of the exceptionally beautiful façade of the university. He read and wrote and taught Latin and Greek and Hebrew, and lectured in Theology; but this immensely private Augustinian found himself at the centre of institutionalised academic jealousy and in-fighting, to the extent that he was imprisoned by the Holy Inquisition for five years for translating (though not publishing) the 'Song of Songs' into Spanish. Some crime, hey?

When they freed him, such was the feeling of expectation in university circles and amongst his students that his lecture room was full to over-flowing on his first day back in work. He took the wind out of their sails with his first words – "As we were saying the other day..." – and was then left in something approaching peace, to an extent, to get back to what he loved best: teaching, and writing poetry and seeking to get very close to God.

He was, at least in terms of literary figures, a contemporary of Saint

162

John of the Cross – they both died in the same year of 1591! – but for us, on the top floor of the Victoria Building, he was much more accessible, even if his themes were the quest for spiritual peace and a oneness with God. Or maybe Stan and I could never get to grips with John, could never understand him, found him far too cerebral for our worldly minds, and gravitated to the slightly easier Odes of Fray Luis (though I don't think, on reflection, that they were all that easy to fathom).

This poet, teacher, philosopher, priest, in many ways encapsulates the spirit of the university city of Salamanca, though he happens to have been born in relatively far-away Cuenca Province, in Castilla-La Mancha. And he has got nothing to do with the city of León, either, so that remains, to me at least, yet another little mystery.

You might want to follow me up this Calle de los Libreros on our way back to the Plaza Mayor, pausing here on the corner of Calle de la Compañía. Lorenzo's going to show us around, but I have to tell you that Lorenzo, always the very best intentioned of guides, a veritable mine of detailed information, chuffed unto his very gutties with his city of Salamanca, never knows when to shut up, bless him. You've paid your guide's fee – though you get the impression that he'd willingly do it all for nothing, for a heartfelt thanks – and, by Jove, he's going to tell you every single thing he knows about the city.

We two are (nominally) in charge of a group of super-shits from north London who loudly profess adoration for and obsession with Saints Teresa de Ávila and Juan de la Cruz. They're here to see every single shrine with even the most minute association with the great mystics. And we two have long since tired of their minimal hold on basic good manners. One of them – a highly obnoxious individual with a wandering eye – has already told me he's reporting me to the London Office because I failed to issue them with a weather forecast for our second day in Teresa's Ávila –

'It's snowing outside, it's February, the temperature is zero, so guess: what d'you think it's going to do tomorrow, dick-head?' should have been my reply – so it comes as no surprise that they have little patience, to say nothing of good manners, towards the little man trying to educate them.

The lay-leader of the group – who swoons every time the utterly out-of-touch, humourless spiritual-leader opens his less than charitable mouth – summons me.

"More walk, less talk."

"Pardon?"

"Tell him we want more walk and less talk."

"I'm not at all sure I know what you mean." I say it slowly so she doesn't miss a word, nor do I have any intention of making this easy for her.

"I would have thought my meaning is obvious. Tell him to stop talking so much. Tell him we can see things for ourselves. Tell him we're not stupid. Tell him to keep moving."

I don't answer, and trust that my look, well practiced over the years with her ilk, will convey my utter contempt. I wait until Lorenzo has finished telling us all he possibly can about the beautiful Casa de las Conchas, now an impressive library, and the huge, gaunt but impressive Universidad Pontificia opposite.

Then I explain to him that Head-Shit Lay-Leader, spokesperson for her fellow-shits, doesn't have the mental or social capability to take in his priceless information, and could we move on as quickly as possible. You won't want to be in their company any longer than necessary, Lorenzo. I'm sure you understand, and my apologies for this lot's social ineptitude. Lorenzo smiles knowingly, takes no offence, takes his own sweet time in finishing, and I feel rather proud of the way I've handled the situation.

But this group, fortunately, was an exception, because nobody can be

164

other than deeply, thankfully affected by Salamanca. Like that wonderful Anglo-Catholic group from East Anglia who managed, by themselves, to explore Salamanca and find the wonderful little Church of Saint Thomas Becket – which I knew nothing about, and I'm the guide! – erected within ten years of his murder, here in west-central Spain. They were delighted with themselves and their discovery, convinced the sacristan to let them celebrate Mass there, went off in search of a good meal afterwards to further celebrate their find.

(Their urbane priest-leader always told us when he 'felt a good meal coming on', and frequently referred to them as occasions when 'I can't remember when I've had more fun when not lying down'.)

And that's what I'm going to let you do, Reader. Go and get a map here on the corner of the Casa de las Conchas from the tiny Tourist Information Office. Up there is the Plaza Mayor, where we started. Behind us a couple of hundred metres are the two cathedrals, the River Tormes and the Roman Bridge. Now, go and get gloriously, joyfully lost in this super, super city, and I'll guarantee you'll end up loving it (almost) as much as Gerard did that first time in the summer of 1995. Then go and tell your friends where you've been and what you've seen. They'll bless you for it.

21. Me and Richard Gere

On his way back to England by road from our little village fifteen kilometres from Pontevedra in the last days of August, 2010, Father John Gerard Feeney somehow managed to convince himself – and Fat Pete, who, receptive to every suggestion, didn't need much convincing, and the dog, oblivious to everything that wasn't food or snoozing – that Terrific Toro was a short cut to the French border. It was nothing of the sort, of course, and he'd have been well advised to come clean and confess that the real reason, flawless and highly commendable in itself, was to load up his luxury camper van with the very best wine that Toro produces (which, of course, he did, thereby depleting Toro's entire stocks by something approaching fifty per cent).

Since Toro doesn't have any campsites – isn't it enough, you'll hasten to say, that what is does have are the best wines in the whole of Spain, and that's a fact: forget about Rioja reds – John decided to push on a little to Tordesillas, where there's an excellent camp site on the very edge of Machado's Duero, looking across that river towards the city. Quiet and sedate, exactly what they were looking for before the long northwards journey the length of France.

So, 'T for Tordesillas' could well have been a distinct possibility at this stage. After all, wasn't it here that the famous treaty to divide South America between Spain and Portugal was signed in 1494, under the auspices and direction of the Pope? And doesn't it justly portray itself as the City of the Treaty, with an excellent museum commemorating that world shattering event? Alan liked it (the museum, that is).

Even if the Main Square is modest in the extreme, and a little bit tired and worn, why shouldn't it be, continuing as it does the centuries' old traditional role of Castilian main squares, a place for social and commercial intercourse, and doing it very well?

And didn't Juana I of Castile, unjustly known as Juana la Loca (Joan the Mad), daughter of Fernando and Isabel, sister of Henry's Catherine of Aragón and rejected wife of Philip the Handsome, in spite of giving him six children, didn't she spend forty-six years here, virtually a prisoner? And wasn't Tordesillas for a while, at least nominally, the capital of Spain by virtue of her residence here?

And modest though it might be, certainly when compared to heavyweights like Sevilla and Salamanca, it nevertheless has much to commend it as a first class example of a typical Castilian provincial town going about its daily business without too much fuss, only too happy to welcome visitors (and two Catholic priests and a dog).

Unfortunately, for worthy Tordesillas, Toledo begins with the same letter of the alphabet, and you simply can't leave out Toledo, can you. No way, Pedro! So we went there to see the Count of Orgaz, and ended up seeing Richard Gere as well.

Leave the car on the outskirts of town, or pay to leave it in an underground parking closer to the centre. Spaniards won't. They'll leave it as close as humanly impossible to their eventual destination, which might be no more than one hundred metres away. That said, and at very long last – except in Galicia, where car-ownership and even minimal intelligence don't go remotely hand-in-hand! – traffic police are actually beginning to move people on or fining them.

Or come by train or bus from wherever you're staying. The service is good, frequent and clean, and both bus and train stations are (by English standards) no great distance away on foot. And walking in has the added advantage of getting a wonderful panoramic view of this quite unique city and appreciating its variation. Make for the Plaza de Zocodover, frequently and mistakenly called the Main Square, though the fact of the matter is that it both looks and performs like a main square. In times gone by it's performed many roles: traditional meeting place for commerce and human interaction, bull ring, and place of execution for those judged to have miffed the Spanish Inquisition in this neck of the woods. Nowadays, it's a joy, a place to see and be seen, to have a Toro red and sit for hours and hours. Sue Wilson would love it.

In form, the square is anything but a square: it's a triangle, attractively paved and planted with shade-giving trees, and it's absolutely snooing at all times of the day and night. Two sides of the triangle are given over to pavement bars and cafes; there are public benches for visitors and tourists to sit and a couple of newspaper kiosks, together with a small Tourist Information Office (there's more elsewhere, by the way, scattered around the city); there's kids running hither and thither in headless-chicken fashion, shouting like Spanish kids are supposed to do, and few complain; people on mobile phones, which they clearly don't need, given the extreme volume of their conversations; and this, being Toledo, there's tourists everywhere you look; and this, being Spain, there's the steady volume of human noise. Opposite the bars and the open air cafes and restaurants, long lines of buses ceaselessly pass along, momentarily complicate forward movement, and eventually wheeze their way up the narrow Cuesta de Carlos V.

(We once stayed in a hotel there – Hotel Carlos V, would you believe, four-star, a lovely place, nice people, eager to please – just down a side alley with a one-in-two slope. Not for the first time we were guiding pilgrims, on this occasion, that nasty, snotty lot from some leafy glade in north London, led by a spiritual director who seemed – even to some of them, his chums! – totally lacking in the milk of human kindness: 'so heavenly blind he was no earthly good', as the unique Johnny Cash once pointedly sang.)

If you carry on towards the top of the Cuesta de Carlos V, on your left, rearing up and dominating the sky-line of Toledo along with the cathedral, is the Alcázar, the scene of exceptional heroism or human stupidity (depending on your point of view) from 21 July, 1936, days after the outbreak of the Spanish Civil War, until 27 September of the same year.

Those loyal to the 'Nacionalistas' – or against the democratically elected, hopelessly organised and deeply flawed, doomed-to-failure Republic: whichever interpretation you prefer – were besieged for ten long, stinkingly hot weeks in this massive four-square fortress. In spite of the pleas of the Republican General Riquelme for him to surrender peacefully, Colonel Moscardó declined, even when his soon-to-be-executed son phoned him. There's a room in the completely renovated Alcázar where the phone conversation reputedly took place, together with photos pertinent to the event, and a (simulated) recording of the tragic conversation.

The almost one thousand active defenders and their families endured aerial and land bombardment for weeks on end, retreating into an ever diminishing enclave of rubble as the massive building was systematically destroyed around their ears. Room-to-room, hand-to-hand fighting, hardly a stone left standing on a stone. Heroic resistance contrasting with efforts to maintain a normal day-to-day existence in abnormal circumstances: a daily newsletter produced on a basic printing machine; operations and amputations by flickering candle-light; celebration of one of the many feasts of the Virgin; a dynamo attached to the back wheel of a motor bike to grind corn; two births recorded and birthdays and anniversaries somehow marked; no electricity and a diminishing supply of drinking water; the walls mined with explosives from the militiamen outside.

Instead of driving on to Madrid – easily the better military option, since Toledo was not in the slightest militarily important – Franco opted for the symbolic alternative and diverted his forces to the relief of the Alcázar. There he was photographed as he strode across the ruined courtyard or over the remains of shattered walls, a small, chubby man, the hero of the hour, the militia now scattered and in retreat. The Army of Africa, victorious and smelling blood, took no prisoners. That wasn't Franco's way, the little shit. It was a huge propaganda coup but it did nothing to shorten the War, which continued for another thirty months.

I went there for the first time in 1960 with Bartomeu and swam in the Tagus (he swam, I paddled and faffed about), then again with Paul and The Class of 1970: John Burke, Kenny, Gerard, Lovely Ronnie Holdsworth

(God rest his soul, which He surely will) and the others. We were impressed. I'm still impressed, though I don't applaud the event. Whatever your political affiliations, it's most certainly worthy of a visit. Like it or loathe it, the Alcázar and its story are fundamental to Toledo.

So, too, is the cathedral.

Juan met us, as arranged, just after ten o'clock in the Plaza del Ayuntamiento, just in front of the Town Hall itself, where there's another Tourist Information Office, and where we two had one of our little tiffs on a previous occasion (brought on by the heat, a lack of coffee, or the fact that we'd inexplicably mislaid a dozen or so of our pilgrims). All around us, in groups big and small and all of them noisy, forming and reforming and bisected by hawkers selling postcards of the cathedral, were sightseers in search of their guides.

Our guide, sunglasses covering half his face, casually dressed with a light jacket draped over his shoulders in spite of the heat, hands in his pockets, knew us from previous occasions, sidled over to us, briefly nodded and greeted us with an American accented "Hi, how you guys today?" Juan's so laid back he's in danger of toppling over, and though he gives the impression that he considers guiding a little bit beneath his dignity, he's very good at it, albeit in unexpected ways.

He doesn't talk much because he thinks too many guides don't know when to stop talking, that they talk tripe. He prefers to speak briefly, tells little stories to lighten the detailed information, humanises the whole event for us, asks the pilgrims questions and encourages them to offer their own answers to his questions. Unlike 'Beatriz of Burgos', he knows what he's talking about, knows what his listeners want, is always keen for his audience to participate in their own education and entertainment.

He also knows the officials on the door of the cathedral, which is a help, and after giving us the briefest of introductions, he takes us inside, tells us to keep up with him, asks us to listen to what he has to say because "I might ask questions at the end!" he adds with the barest hint of a smile, leaving you wondering if he means it.

It's a truly massive monument of architectural achievement. The first stone was laid in 1226, and more than two hundred and sixty years later – not a misprint – in 1493, it was finished, which goes some considerable way to explain its mélange of styles: pure French Gothic, mudéjar, and Plateresque. It is, quite simply, a truly majestic cathedral, from its side-chapels to its High Altar to its Choir to its Cloisters to its Sacristy, the latter a treasure-trove in itself, its walls hung with El Greco's masterpieces of the twelve apostles, its altarpiece crowned with the quite exceptional 'Denuding of Christ'.

I know that cathedrals and churches in general arouse different reactions in different people (which is as it should be: most Anglican pilgrims we know find Burgos Cathedral an architectural step too far), but there can be few religious buildings anywhere – not just in Spain – which can rival the Cathedral of Toledo for the sheer intensity and breadth of its architectural achievement. It was meant to have two matching spires, but someone lost the plans so they were stuck with one (I think). Still, it's a beauty. Juan likes it very much, though he doesn't appear overly excited. Juan doesn't do overly excited except when he moves into second gear when he talks about his little son.

After an hour or so, he leaves us, reminding us he'll meet us later in the morning to continue the tour. You can't rush Toledo, he says, and points us in the general direction of the Jewish Quarter. Just ramble at will, he advises us, and let chance take us down unsuspected alleys and side-streets.

It's all a matter of opinion, of course, as it should be, but to us two the best part of the city, and the quietest, has always been the Jewish

Quarter in the west, so we needed no telling. It's brimming with atmosphere, with that something which can't be explained by mere words, which can only be felt, architectural gems scattered about hither and thither, back alleys and back streets so narrow the sun never shines on them, courtyards and balconies and flowers and coolness and peace, no more than a couple of hundred metres at very most from the noise and bustle of Zocodover, yet a world away.

And here, whatever else you do, don't under any circumstances miss the Sinagoga de Santa María la Blanca. It is, in a word, stunning, and it defies adequate description, an architectural mixture of the utterly simple and the exceptionally intricate, with its white horse-shoe arches and plasterwork. Sadly, in 1391, the peace and mutual respect that had existed between faiths was shattered when the Jews were massacred on this very spot.

Nothing deterred by man's hatred of man, and by the fact that history seemingly teaches us nothing of lasting value, go along the Calle de los Reyes Católicos (remember them?) and stop at the Sinagoga of Samuel Levy (more commonly known as the 'Tránsito'). As with Santa María la Blanca, nothing about the outside of the building will in any way prepare you for the exceptional ornamental richness of the interior. It's just fabulous: intricately hand-carved ceilings of larch wood, sumptuously decorated walls and friezes. And within the synagogue is the Museum of Sephardi (Spanish Jewish) culture in the form of manuscripts, costumes, and sacred objects of worship, a reminder of the indescribable debt Spain owes to the Jewish – and Muslim – legacy.

You could happily spend entire days in this part of the city of the great El Greco, whose house (and museum), by the way, is literally just around the corner from the 'Tránsito'. Like so very much of Toledo, it's simply unmissable, but, on this occasion, we had to head to our first meeting place, the Plaza del Ayuntamiento, for the second part of the tour with Juan. He looks refreshed – not that he ever looks remotely flustered, mind you – and he's probably spent the last hour with his little son, because he brings him and his wife to meet us. The grannies in the group start to drool.

He suggests we might want to follow him, and he sets off at a gentle pace – how else! – down the Calle del Salvador, which eases into the Calle de Santo Tomé. He gathers the group in the little square in front of the church of the same name, asks them if they can all hear him, and tells them succinctly about what they're going to see whilst I go and get the discounted tickets.

Just inside the door and before you enter the church proper, there, on your right, where everybody's stopped, looking at the wall, is arguably the most celebrated painting El Greco ever executed in his illustrious career, set back behind a railing. It was painted on this very wall, it's never been moved, never been restored. It is as it was some four hundred plus years ago.

It's called 'El Entierro del Conde de Orgaz' ('The Burial of the Count of Orgaz'). Commissioned by the parish priest and painted in 1586, it depicts the burial, in 1323, of Gonzalo Ruíz de Toledo, a philanthropist, a nobleman of pious and exemplary virtue throughout his life. In the foreground, supported by Saints Stephen and Augustine, the count is laid to rest. Behind him and the two saints, painted in sixteenth century costume, are those who have come to pray for his soul. Saints and noblemen (and the little lad on the left, El Greco's son) are all identifiable, contemporary men of worth and standing, all personally known to the painter and to Toledo of that time. Above them, in what you might call the 'second half' of the painting, the soul of the count is received into Heaven.

Such a description, for what it's worth, can only distantly hint at the exceptional degree of quality and meaning of the painting.

Juan, who's seen it countless times, loves it. I, who have seen it many times (the first time with Bartomeu, surprise, surprise!) love it, and I look around at the groups held in awe by its beauty and meaning.

I turn around slowly and a metre behind me stands a man of slightly more than average height, an old-fashioned, baggy, peaked cap carelessly askew on his greying head, National Health spectacles on his nose, unshaven for what must be a few days, to judge from the stubble, wearing an old jacket which hinted at being some indeterminate shade of brown, a pair of jeans, scuffed shoes. I greet him.

"Good morning. Aren't you Richard Gere? Nice to see you."

Two unnaturally muscled men above two metres in height and almost as wide move forward imperceptibly.

"Yes, I am. How are you?"

I tell him it's very nice to see him, that I'll detain him no further, and tell him to have a nice day. I want to ask him what it's like to get that close to Julia Roberts, but I'll leave that until the next time we two meet in the Church of Santo Tomé in Toledo. I move off and round up the group of women-of-a-certain-age, their lower jaws dropped, another-worldly look on their faces, the Count of Orgaz already relegated to a very distant second place.

Outside in the sun, those who aren't briefly nursing bloodied knees as a result of falling down the steps on their way out of the church look at each other wordlessly, then jabber all at once. Juan thinks, rightly, that he might as well finish the tour here and now. He's lost them to Dickie.

The appearance of Richard Gere apart, you have to ask yourself if there is a more completely satisfying city in all Spain (Sevilla included), and you know you'll have to come back, that you haven't seen enough. Rainer María Rilke, whose name and fame will probably outlast Dickie, wrote in a letter to a chum in 1912: "You cannot begin to imagine the wonder of this city." You're right there, pal.

(The Caja Rural de Toledo has published, in Spanish and English, a free, exceptionally well produced, exquisitely photographed little booklet on this very work of art. This is, in part, how it explains in translation a section of the painting: 'The vestments are awe inspiring due to their resolution from the transparency on the cleric's surplice, a prodigy of oil based diluted brush-strokes to the gold and silk embroidery, on the Augustine's pluvial and Stephen's dalmatic.' Make of that what you will. The translator's name has been sensibly omitted.)

And the best view of the city? Go up to the Parador of Toledo on the other side of the almost completely encircling River Tagus, cleaving its way westwards through Extremadura to Lisbon and the Atlantic. Find the long balcony that looks across at the city. Look from left to right and back again as many times as you feel inclined, forget the fact that you're fast becoming giddy, make up your own mind, and come back and tell us what you think.

Go on! Bet we won't be able to shut you up once you get started! Don't be embarrassed! We're all on your side! That's what Toledo does to you!

22. María del Carmen Marín Moreno

I clearly recall the month and the year: July, 1988. The exact date of the month I'm not so sure about, but it must have been within the first ten days of the month, since internal summer examinations were over, reports had been written, and there was a general air of relaxation and comparative lack of tension in the air with the seven weeks of summer holidays just over the horizon. I also remember it because it effectively brought to a close the end of what had generally become known as The Brezhnev Years at Saint Mary's College, Crosby, Liverpool L23 5TW. Not the Russian version, you understand, but our own period when, finally, the stultifying reign of fourteen years of the humourless Irish-born headmaster was almost over.

Not that we had all that much to look forward to, since his successor, already into his sixties and in much less than perfect health, had a reputation for opening his mouth without sufficient pre-thought, and saying the first thing that came into his mind, usually a curt order or a few chosen words of unadorned criticism of one sort or another. Where one had been frigid and with little discernible ember of human warmth, the other was to be belligerent, combative, and insensitive. Or, to put it rather more bluntly, a bully. You won't be surprised to learn that we didn't get on.

For years Geoff and I had been asking the humourless one to consider giving the Spanish Department a Spanish Language Assistant. For years he'd tied me up in verbal knots by talking around the matter, or referring to an entirely different thing, hoping I'd go away. For some inexplicable reason in late May, when it was officially too late to do anything about it, some six weeks before his dream-like reign petered out, he approached me on the fifth form corridor and muttered his unexpected approval. We immediately went through the motions, with no great hopes, and all but forgot about it.

Back to the first ten days of July, 1988.

I was in the secretary's office looking for something or other when the telephone chanced to ring, not a totally unexpected event, you'll quickly remind me, given the location. The secretary, a small woman with a ready reply and an astronomical opinion of her own worth, who thought she ran the school single-handed, and didn't particularly like mere teachers to be in her holy of holies for any reason, became unusually flustered. Seeing me loitering there, she told me, with no great show of friendliness, that the call seemed to be for me, from what little she could decipher coming distantly from the other end. She held out the phone at arm's length as if it offended her.

It was María del Carmen Marín Moreno, and she was calling from Úbeda (Ubbada, its original name in Arabic). She was sorry for this late-in-the-term, last-minute call. She wondered if the post of Spanish Language Assistant was still vacant. I assured her that it was, that I would immediately speak with my (outgoing) headmaster, and would she please telephone me at this number in thirty minutes.

I spoke to him, she rang back in thirty minutes, and we gleefully agreed to employ her – on a pittance – from the start of September. I gave her my number to arrange matters for her accommodation and arrival, and Geoff and I got ready to welcome her. The fact that the new head in September openly resented a decision made by his predecessor which he'd have to honour – I suppose he had a point, when you come to think of it – made not the slightest difference to our mood, though it would subsequently spoil things for the very people it was designed to help in the study of Spain's lovely language.

María – she preferred that name rather than the more usual Mari Carmen – was in her early twenties. Impeccably dressed in the latest designer-jeans, she was as suitably dark as any Andalusian should be, with a blemish-free face which tapered to a markedly pointed chin. She was a great help, though she missed home rather more than you'd have expected from someone her age, with the result that she went back to Úbeda at every opportunity. The only thing we found difficult to accept was her slovenly Andalusian accent, and we tried, unsuccessfully, to get her to change the habits of a limited lifetime, and to speak 'proper' Spanish, Castilian Spanish, don't you know. In June the following year, her nephew came to stay with us for two weeks in flat Formby by the cold Irish Sea.

Bernardo was markedly Teutonic in appearance, all flaxen haired and blue eyed, rimless spectacles. He seemed to find everything something of a chore, from merely breathing to adapting marginally to English food – we invariably ate Mediterranean, to no effect – to getting up before noon. He was a nice enough lad in the sense that he wasn't in any way unpleasant, but he was not by nature – or practice, perhaps? – positive or active or optimistic. You were glad he was somebody else's son.

Later that summer, leaving Catherine to starve for a week or so in Suances with Angelina and her family, we two drove a slightly reluctant Simon from northerly Santander to southerly Úbeda, almost seven hundred blazing kilometres, chasing the clouds for minimal shade, where he stayed for two weeks with the listless Bernardo. And that's how we two got to know Úbeda for the first time. Some twenty years later, with the ubiquitous Barbara and Alan, and based in nearby Baeza, we went there for the second time.

We English often imagine Andalucía to be populated by preposterously beautiful, black-eyed, black-haired women with a rose clamped between teeth of incomparable whiteness, full of bust, with voluminous dresses in the most iridescent colours, snapping their fingers and castanets, stamping their high-heeled feet in some sort of apparent unison, a sneer for a smile, looking, if anything, angry with someone or something unidentifiable. Their men are beautifully proportioned, slicked-back hair, pencil-thin moustache, gliding effortlessly around their women, clapping their hands and prancing around like arseholes, whilst somebody behind him, seated on a cheap chair, is strumming the very be-jaysus out of a guitar, a companion alongside singing as if he's being castrated without an anaesthetic.

And then there's bullfighting, of course, that affront to civilised behaviour, all blood and sand and death in the afternoon.

You'll be happy – or disappointed? – to know that it's not (all) like that at all, whatever you've been led to believe by Andalusians and non-Spaniards alike.

Úbeda is an elegant town which seems to owe more to its Renaissance legacy than anything else. It doesn't look particularly southern or gypsy or flamenco-obsessed (but it is bloody hot in the summer). This town of thirty-five thousand is monumental like very few others in the whole of the Peninsula, and its monuments, in the vast majority of cases, are decidedly Renaissance, in spite of its eight centuries of close proximity to an alien culture: it's got relatively little to show, architecturally speaking, for eight hundred years of Moorish conquest.

Its present, of course, owes everything to its variegated history. It's situated in the geographical centre of the Province of Jaén. In the bewildering to-ing and fro-ing of Christian and Muslim advances and retreats, it was to become, from the middle of the thirteenth century, a frontier against the invaders; and the Christian kings of Castilla and their successors, seeing its importance as a bulwark, granted it privileges and concessions, built castles and palaces, and set about the architectural Christianisation of the town.

I have not the slightest inclination to give you a list of palaces and stately homes and museums and churches and convents: it's reckoned that there are more than two hundred and fifty of them (and that's a fact). If interested, you can look them up for yourself, Reader. But that very number, of itself, should give you a good idea that it's not remotely like the English conception of what a southern Spanish town should be, thank God.

Nowadays, fifty per cent of its inhabitants find employment – where employment can be found in these dark days of 2012, Zapatero now little more than a nasty taste still in the mouth – in commerce and local administration and the good-old service industries, all of which seems to be slightly at odds with the town's architectural worth, its history, its culture. And in spite of such a plethora of beauty, the town's worthies only rate the possibility of 'turismo culto' as 'incipiente'. I cannot believe it. Somebody with influence and clout somewhere in Úbeda needs to get his or her finger out and sell this exceptional town to the visitors, starting with Spaniards. You could stay here a week and still not see all there is to see.

And, of course, this being a town in that huge mass of land known as Andalucía, you won't be surprised to know that the cultivation of olives, producing some fifteen per cent of the world's olive production, is important, to say the least. Here, as in nearby Baeza and Jaén, thousands and thousands and thousands of olive trees march in battalion order over hill and dale, dipping and diving fluidly, creating a heady maze of patterns against the yellow-ochre soil, before disappearing in a distant heat haze to an unseen horizon.

I'm left to agree that it's no wonder María del Carmen Marín Moreno was so keen to leave the allure of Crosby every chance she got all those twenty-something years ago. Úbeda and Crosby are what we might confidently term 'no contest', I'm sure you'll wholeheartedly agree.

23. The Door of Pardon

Margaret and I very much like Villafranca del Bierzo. Thank God we've got something in common! Joke! Joke! Honest to God! Just wanted to get your attention, that's all. Oh, hell! Why did I ever mention it! Let's start again on a more positive, diplomatic note, shall we? Here we go.

Villafranca del Bierzo, with its population of just short of four thousand good souls, is in the extreme north-west of Castilla-León, west of sprawling Ponferrada, in the Sierra de Ancares, in the province of León, the proverbial stone's throw from Galicia's eastern border, on the A6 to Lugo (though why you'd want to go to Lugo beats us two, Benavente thankfully an equal distance behind you). The small town's got four churches, three convents and a monastery, and it's a very important stage on the Road to Santiago de Compostela, to which, in no small measure, it owes its birth and development and, in all probability, its present-day economy.

(How's that for a less polemic start, then?)

We went to the Colegiata, the Collegiate Church, for the Saturday evening Vigil Mass. We had to leave early the next morning, wanting to get back to the grandchildren. Originally, it was founded in the eleventh century by the influential French monks of far away Cluny as a monastery, and the present Colegiata was built on the remains of that Monasterio de Santa María de Cluny. It took two centuries to complete!

It's actually a lovely building, both inside and outside, though it looks considerably larger outside than inside, daft though that might seem. Inside, the upward proportions and girth of the columns are so enormous as to render space for the faithful at something of a premium, and the height of the roof is simply celestial. But it's attractive, it's full to overflowing with grannies in their heavy winter coats against the February cold; and there's a few men, too, just for the record, but they're so ridiculously outnumbered as to appear totally insignificant. There's a few young people here, perhaps as many as the numerically insignificant men. Maybe there was nowhere else for them to go that Saturday night. Maybe the absentees are saving themselves for Sunday Mass! As if! Let's not forget that this is 'Catholic Spain'. Spot the cleverly concealed sarcasm, did you?

The fact of the matter is that since the dictator Franco (as he's now correctly known) eventually popped his clogs in November 1975, and probably long before, the number of practising Catholics in Spain – those going to Mass on Sundays and Holy Days – has steadily declined, and is now about eighteen per cent. That's not a misprint. (I keep saying that, don't I?)

I once had occasion to mention this in passing in an initially friendly conversation with one of our guides in Segovia and she nearly had a fit, protesting that Spain was more Catholic than the Vatican, that the Catholic Faith was at the very core of all aspects of Spanish life. The English priest from Runcorn, Cheshire, who was with our Pax Travel pilgrims, sagely nodded his agreement with my remarks, and we two instantly became 'personae non gratae' with Severely Miffed of Segovia, who was quite clearly seeing life through the rosiest of rose-tinted spectacles. The guided tour was never quite the same after that. Still, the truth must out, as they say.

But I've simply got to tell you this, though it may have little or nothing directly to do with Villafranca del Bierzo, other than the fact that I saw the article in ABC's edition of February 13, 2011 (and again, in a slightly shorter form on the same day in 'Público'). I was in the pleasant sitting room of Villafranca's pleasant parador, all tastefully updated in bright, pastel shades, friendly people on reception, and everywhere else, come to think of it. Pauline and Henry simply adore it, ask us to take them there more often.

Both newspapers reported an event of singular importance in the general fabric of Spanish society, which has become more and more laicised, less and less interested and involved in religious matters over the last fifty years or so. In the majestic Cathedral of Burgos, in early February of 2011, no fewer than one hundred and eighty-one young women, all of them under the age of thirty-five, almost all of them university (or similarly) educated, all of them having made their mark in commercial or educational or other professional areas throughout Spain, were welcomed into the new religious order of the Instituto de Iesu Communio.

Beaming faces, eyes aglow, utterly aware of the implications of their choice, they were received as cloistered nuns into this order based in the nearby town of Lerma. And the great and the good of the Spanish Catholic Church were there in force to greet them and to celebrate this event: the Archbishop of Burgos, Francisco Gil Hellín; the President of the Episcopal Conference, Cardinal Antonio María Rouco Varela; the Archbishop of Pamplona, together with the Bishop-elect of Ciudad Rodrigo, Raúl Berzosa. German Benedict, to indicate his blessings and whole-hearted agreement, even sent his nuncio, Renzo Fratini.

And, much more importantly, perhaps, and putting the situation into a more human, credible context, the newly professed nuns were surrounded by parents and families and friends and other well-wishers, unabashedly sharing their manifest joy (and, according to reporter Vanessa Pi, there's another hundred or so youngsters on the waiting list).

It's all down to Sor (Sister) Verónica Berzosa – yes, you guessed, the sister of the Bishop-elect of Ciudad Rodrigo – a charismatic forty-four year old, who gave up her university studies at the age of eighteen, opting for the contemplative life. She's beyond doubt the leading light, a woman of tremendous personal dedication and attraction, charismatic, as they say, with a crystal-clear view of her vocation.

And my point is this: at a time when Spain and Spaniards continue to slip further and further away from their sacramental duties; when divorce and co-habitation and abortions are on the up and up; when Spaniards no longer look towards the Church for moral guidance; when Zapatero's last ten years in power have bare-facedly and aggressively pursued an open policy of putting the Catholic Church in Spain in its rightful place – as he sees it – here we have a significant conservative backlash on a grand scale, led by young women (and their friends and families and well-wishers). Frankly, it's hard to explain. And you can add to this a similar contemplative order, admittedly smaller, equally young, called the Blue Nuns, living (and working) in their convent in the very shadow of Oropesa's formidable parador (Margaret's favourite!), west of Toledo. We two have witnessed their joy in their chosen vocation on our countless visits there. It's pure, natural, unadulterated joy, nothing less, believe you me.

Quite naturally, Sor Verónica's sisters are not everybody's cup of tea, and there are more 'progressive' sectors in the Catholic Church in Spain who view them with a certain suspicion (and jealousy, perhaps?). And whilst, as a practising Catholic prone to sin, I personally welcome this initiative, I have to wonder if its appeal will extend to and influence the mass of Catholics (of various persuasions and intensity) in Spain. I fervently hope so. Will it, in their day to day lives, get any more youngsters actively involved? Or, when the present crop of grannies and token males pass on, will the churches – like the one in Villafranca del Bierzo, where we attended the Saturday Vigil Mass: remember? – become increasingly empty until they close their doors or merge? I repeat: I hope the outcome will be positive. There's simply got to be an alternative to the 15-minutes-of-fame dick-heads who are considered, euphemistically, 'celebrities', taking their cue from the Americans, whom we still allow to dictate morality. There's got to be. Otherwise, we're all doomed to less than mediocrity by an increasingly brain-dead minority.

But here's the other side of things. It's the first Sunday of August, 2011, and our little church in Tourón is packed to the very rafters (which are not as high as Villafranca's!). There's a baptism this morning. The parents, little more than teenagers – or am I getting old? – obviously have not been in a church in recent memory. They're looking around, trying to get their bearings, wondering what's going on, talking and chewing gum. Our priest has started the Mass with three – three! Jesus! – separate

187

novenas: one to the local Virgin, the second to San Roque, and the third to the Vírgen del Pilar, and eventually he starts the Mass, after singing every hymn the congregation of grannies knows (all in different keys, of course, though somehow harmoniously). The homily consists of the re-telling of the three Readings, which, by the way, are self explanatory.

(Stop there a second: can anybody tell me, by the by, why there's so much devotion and so many novenas to San Roque in Spain? He was French, born in Montpellier! Or maybe it's the even more obscure San Roque, a Jesuit priest and martyr, born in Paraguay? I don't think so. The mystery remains unexplained, then.)

There's a kid of six or seven across the aisle from me behaving badly, and I would happily take him outside and give him a bloody good hiding. He tells his ultra patient grandmother: "Yo me aburro" ("I'm bored stiff"), and you see the kid in a different light. Of course he's bloody well bored stiff, because there's nothing here for anybody under sixty-five years of age! Have the Spaniards never heard of 'Little Church'? There simply has got to be a change of attitudes to engage kids and adolescents. The alternative is stark: there won't be any church-goers within twenty years. Mark my words.

I know an English priest of sixty-one years of age. The kids in downtown, deprived Birkenhead hang on his every word. The parents love and support him (even if the Bishop doesn't like him all that much!). He doesn't talk rubbish, doesn't dilute the message: he engages them. He talks to them in a language they understand, without ever talking down to them. Tells them about Everton and the love of God. Tells them they're precious in God's sight. Tells them Jesus loves them and there's nothing they can do that'll make Him stop loving them. Jesus wept! Surely to God it's not that hard to make a change, not that hard to make things relevant? Father Leo, aged seventy plus, did it in Formby. Surely it's time to appreciate that change is the only alternative? Good-Jesus-Tonight!

But let's get back to Villafranca del Bierzo (before I really do blow a fuse), in the extreme north-west corner of Castilla-León, west of sprawling Ponferrada, in the Sierra de Ancares, in the province of León, the proverbial stone's throw from the Galician border, Pauline and Henry's favourite parador ("Can we go again soon?").

It's a lovely place to visit and stay, but, of course, such places are all the better (and only really matter) when the company's good and the memories flood. There was that group from Runcorn with Pax Travel: they were a superb lot, one and all. Superb examples of what Catholics should be. Superb examples of what Christians should be.

We'd met them in Madrid's airport, and from there until we returned them to Barajas one week later, they sang every song they knew – and some they didn't! – from The Superb Sixties.

"No, no, listen. D'you ever 'member that one that goes ..."

"Bet none of youse can get this one, though. Bet you a quid you won't."

"You hum it, I'll sing it, then."

"Worra 'bout this one from Cilla Black, eh? Bet no-one knows that right through to the very end."

And so it went on. So it will come as no great surprise to you to be told that on the leg from León (via Astorga) to Villafranca, they were still singing (in between spontaneous group Rosary sessions, equally vociferous) when the bus dropped us off alongside the gardens of the Alameda, in the north end of this compact town.

"Oh, is this it, then? We're here, are we, already? Come on, girls, let's gerroff before we're thrown off, then. What time? What time did he say we're leaving, again? Half past what? Where we eatin' then, girls?"

And so it went on, wonderful, natural humour, innocent candour, instant friendship, singing and praying and laughing (and crying, too).

We eventually managed to walk them to the Main Square, five minutes away, but already strung out in a long, noisy line, somebody or other running back to the bus.

"Hang on. I've left me thingy on the bus an' it might rain, you never know, do you? Just wait a mo'."

We showed them where to eat on the Main Square and told them we two would meet them in the square an hour and a half from now to show them around the walkable town of Villafranca del Bierzo (which produces some truly excellent wines, you might want to know).

"Where we meeting, then. Back at the bus?"

"No. He said 'ere. Didn't you hear him? You mustn't've been listening, you."

"What time, then?"

"Same as he said. In an hour and a half."

"When's that, then?"

And so it went on.

We two slipped away to the tiny, below-ground-level Mesón Don Nacho, down a side-alley importantly called Calle Trúqueles, which is so narrow it doesn't appear on the very good official street map we got from the Information Office opposite the Alameda. Stretch out both arms and you'll be able to touch both walls of what's nothing more than a back alley; couldn't swing a cat in it without rendering it senseless. It's run by a corpulent but friendly lad of about twenty-five, and two portly Costa Rican ladies, neither of whom quite clearly have time for unnecessary chit-chat, and don't suffer fools gladly, but their food is stunning, in simplicity and taste and quantity.

We went in and I stood at the bar. The pear-shaped young man standing next to me was admiring the back page of 'Diario As'. He farted companionably, coughed politely (or was it the other way around?), smiled a greeting, wished me a nice day, and returned to his study of the back page of 'Diario As'. I asked one of the ladies for a table for two. Recognising us from countless previous visits, she smiled briefly and nodded her head – which, for her, were signs of unbridled enthusiasm – and wordlessly pointed us to a table in the corner.

Minutes later, half a dozen Runcornites – or whatever they call themselves – having tracked us down, came in, and, using Scouse as the 'lingua franca', together with a multitude of internationally recognised gestures, somehow succeeded in getting themselves seated and served. The meal, the company, the location were perfect. Again.

Back in the Main Square, half an hour late – them, not us two: perish the thought! – the Liverpool-born priest in charge said they'd all like to walk a bit of the Road to Santiago if that were possible: he said he'd heard it passed through Villafranca del Bierzo. Before lunch, it looked as though they were in no condition to walk anywhere. After lunch they were somehow sufficiently fortified, all of them, to hike up the steep Calle de San Jerónimo, passing the enormous Church of San Francisco, rearing up on the left; managed to keep their feet on the precipitous downward slope and then on past the Calle Campo de la Gallina ("'Ere, Lil, just give us yer 'and an' I'll be fine, will you!"); stopped for breath and another hilarious conversation before climbing the steps to something that just about passed for a track, the Calle de Santiago.

And there it is, the Church of Santiago, a Romanesque, single-nave construction, built in 1186, with its famous Puerta de Perdón.

Reliable tradition has it that those pilgrims unable to go further by dint of illness or exhaustion, could, with the local bishop's permission, take Holy Communion as they knelt at the side door – not the front – of the church. They would then be deemed to have completed the entire pilgrimage to Santiago de Compostela and worthy of the same spiritual benefits as those who actually walked the journey from start to finish.

We told our group and they were suitably and respectfully impressed. We went inside and each prayed in his own manner. And the occasion got to a dozen or so of them, these singers and jokers and laughter-makers, as they laid their personal troubles at the altar. Two sons, who had inexplicably committed suicide, whose parents had never properly grieved, the father of one crying on Margaret's shoulder, the first time he'd really shared his grief with anyone, not even his wife, we were later told; those in remission from one form or another of cancer; those with personal problems that had long scarred their lives and were still a presence; those with sons and daughters who had somehow gone wrong; those for whom life seemed unnaturally hard and going nowhere.

Silent tears and deeply bowed heads, private and briefly oblivious to those around them; pent up feelings bravely controlled; an arm around the shoulders for support; a handkerchief quietly passed; a look of compassion from those few left unscarred. Honest people talking to their God, in whom they confided. No statues of a copiously bleeding Christ and a Mother at the very end of her tether. Just honest-to-God trust and love: not a Spanish thing, I'm afraid. It was good to be part of it, to be tacitly reminded of what was really important, not the fact that we were almost two hours behind time and would arrive in Santiago de Compostela later than planned. I phoned ahead and they told me it was no problem in Hotel Gelmírez. Saint James and Villafranca were working their miracles again, looking after us.

Only slightly subdued, but somehow fortified in spite of their on-going sorrows, they fell over the steps and out into the mid afternoon sun, past the two pilgrims' 'albergues' where we two had exchanged a greeting with two beaming Japanese pilgrims in torrential rain three months previously.

On down the hill we went – and where, pray tell, isn't there a hill in Villafranca del Bierzo! – and on past the enormous bulk of the Castillo de Villafranca, now a private residence.

"Oh, it's a castle, is it? Nice. It's all right for some."

Down and down until we reached Calle del Agua, a pilgrims' street, with its palaces and stately homes and mansions and its family shields left and right, all in various states of decay and renovation, and we tried to translate the history of the place for our group and give it a human face, give them a taste of Villafranca's past. We could happily live here.

Then, it was belatedly back on the bus, but nobody cared about the delay, not even the driver. They tipped him handsomely and spoke to him in Scouse. He looked at their eyes and their smiles and he understood them perfectly.

We wound our way tortuously back across the River Burbia, up Calle Concepción and Calle Espíritu Santo on the outskirts of the town, waved to real, live pilgrims, met up with the A6 which took us past Lugo (without a sideways glance of recognition, of course).

"No real point stopping there, girls. It's a right dump, honest to God. That okay with you, Father?"

They're singing again.

"Hey, listen. No, listen, hush a minute. Anyone here know all the words to 'Needles and Pins', then? Come on, somebody must. I'll sing the first verse, eh?"

24. Wamba

If you thought there was a dearth of places in Spain beginning with the letter K (and that's the Basque spelling, rather than the Castilian, remember), spare a thought for the letter W. There's just one – yes, one – it's called Wamba, and it's geographically more or less in the centre of the irregularly shaped province of Valladolid, itself due north-north-west of Madrid's climatically challenged capital.

This same Valladolid, quite naturally, is the capital of the province of

Valladolid, and the 370 or so good souls who live in Wamba, seventeen kilometres from Valladolid, call themselves 'wambareños'. Not many people outside of Wamba know that, so you, Reader, are in possession of a fact of some significance! Congratulations!

With the greatest respect to all 'wambareños', its past is infinitely more important than its present, more important than its future ever will be.

Apparently – and you've got to be careful here, Spanish legends being what they are – legend has it that in 672, the inhabitants of an isolated community in this neck of the woods elected their own king (a novelty for those, or any, times). His name was Wamba – nothing to do with the fool in 'Ivanhoe', but who knows, legends being legends – and the name stuck. Little if anything is known about Wamba, the settlement, other than the fact that a Visigothic church, perhaps with some involvement from the ubiquitous Cistercian monks of French Cluny, was erected there.

It was called Santa María de Wamba. Little of the original building was ever found or recorded – thus immediately imbuing it with the status of legend, and, perhaps, some doubt – but it's generally assumed and accepted that the present church of the same name was reconstructed in the twelfth century on the original mozarabic church by the Knights Hospitaler (who go under a variety of names: the Knights of Saint John, for instance, better known as the Order of the Knights of Malta).

Still with me? Honestly? Well done!

Now, I don't want to swamp you with unexplained facts, but let's tarry a while for me to explain something, to wit, the word 'mozarabic'

In the year 711, hordes of disciplined, ambitious Arabs of various persuasions invaded Spain with embarrassing ease, moving like an unobstructed tidal wave northwards throughout the entire peninsula – and one or two places in Galicia: too far and too wet! – eventually reaching well beyond the Pyrenees and into France. Thereafter, they fairly quickly settled back into conquered Spain. Over the next (almost) eight hundred years, they slowly withdrew southwards until they mainly occupied what is now Andalucía, from which they were belatedly ejected in 1492. This much you know, if you've been paying attention in the earlier part of this book, but I thought it worth refreshing your memory and putting things into context.

In the main, there had been no 'them' and 'us', but rather an accommodation in most things, with certain exceptions, as you might expect, as when fanatics on one side or the other seemed determined to annihilate the opposing religious tendencies. Nothing new there, then!

The descendents of the Iberian Christians who lived under the Islamic rule of Al Andalus didn't convert to Islam, but they did adopt (and adapt) elements of Arabic culture: literature, language and, of course, architecture. The outcome of this artistic fusion was called 'mozarabic', and is characterised by architectural sobriety, considerable technique, and, most especially, the horse-shoe arch.

Right, so that, briefly – ahem! – is what 'mozarabic' means. Feel better for knowing that, do you? So now we can get back to Wamba and the church of Santa María de Wamba.

As you might expect, it is simplicity itself. There's what we'll call a tomb, inside of which rest no fewer than three thousand skulls belonging to monks who helped bring and establish Christianity in this isolated region; and on one of the walls, there's the following inscription:

Como te ves, yo me vi.
Como me ves, te verás.
Todo acaba en esto aquí.
Piénsalo y no pecarás.

196

As now you see yourself, I once saw myself.
As you now see me, so will you see yourself.
Everything ends in this way here on earth.
So dwell on that and you will sin no more.

Well, now! It loses just a little in translation, as all poetry must, but you get the message, I'm sure.

And a last gem of information for your edification.

Urraca of Portugal – 'urraca' means 'magpie', by the way – quondam wife of Fernando II of León, married him when she was fourteen years of age. Shortly thereafter, finding out that they were second cousins by marriage (which had never occurred to either party before the marriage!), Fernando got Pope Alexander III to annul the marriage. Poor Urraca retired to the monastic life, firstly in the province of nearby Zamora, and ultimately to the Monastery – as the church was then called – of Santa María de Wamba.

Interesting, eh?

25. Xinzo de Limia

I know this is bound to sound something like an excuse – which, by the way, it certainly isn't – but there's only slightly more than forty places in all Spain (three in nearby Portugal) beginning with the letter 'X' (and a few of them can also be written with 'J' instead of 'X', just to complicate matters even further). Here's a random list of them for you to choose from (and the provinces where they're located):

Xátiva	(Valencia)	Xesteira (Pontevedra)
Xiá	(Lugo)	Xixona (Alicante)
Xuño	(La Coruña)	Xendive (Ourense)

So, in all honesty, how many of them did you recognise for even the slightest reason (and I haven't chosen these five to prove a point, either, if that's what you're thinking)?

The only one we two even remotely know is Xinzo de Limia, and the main reason for that – nay, the one, solitary reason for that – is because on the countless road journeys we've made over the last fifteen years between Barajas Airport, Madrid, and Galicia, in Spain's green and pleasant north-west (where we now live, thank God for all His mercies!), we've had to pass Xinzo de Limia. Let's face it, unless you fly the same journey, there's no way of not passing Xinzo de Limia.

Furthermore, for your information, 'pass it' is just about all you do (and by the end of this necessarily brief chapter you'll understand the reason for so doing). I could have cheated, by the way, and introduced you to Xavier, but that's just a castle, where the great Spanish Jesuit and missionary, San Francisco Xavier, was born. It was also the ancestral seat of the very important Xavier family. And, if you've stayed with me right to the (almost) bitter end of the Spanish alphabet's twenty-seven letters, cheating is something I just couldn't do to you! We've been through a lot together, you and I, Reader!

Behind us is the embarrassingly ordinary Benavente, which, fortunately, we don't have to pass through. From the road you're presented with what seem miles and miles of land strewn with farming equipment of every size and shape – surely more than the whole of Spain needs – most of it for sale or hire, some of it the worse for the weather. So, from the very outset, the potential visitor is discouraged from exploring Benavente further. Even the parador is disappointing, sad to say, overlooking a cement factory far below (as you'll remember, if you've been paying attention).

Nothing deterred and thanking God for not detaining us further, we sweep on to Puebla de Sanabria. Oft times we've tarried there for much more than a while, and it's a lovely place to visit. The main part of the small town is built on a precipitous hill which you really shouldn't attempt to climb if you've got a dicky ticker (or obese, in the fashion of many Spanish males). Most Spaniards we meet either drive up the one-in-two one-hundred-metre slope to the postage stamp sized Main Square, or take one look at it from below and decide not to bother, which is a pity, since the views are spectacular and the town is pleasingly quaint, full of little unexpected oddities which make you smile and glad you stayed (but it's face-numbingly cold in the winter months). The lovely family of the lovely Ana Lobato lives here.

Reluctantly, after the usual coffee and a wee and a walk around familiar landmarks, we drive westwards past featureless A Gudiña (where we once had a stupendous customised, while-you-wait pizza the size of a bin lid) ready for the huge sweep of the A-52 as it passes – but sensibly never enters – Verín. As you'll know from previous comments, it's one of those few places in Spain – Vilaba, in Lugo province, is another – where we've tried very hard, and spectacularly failed, to find anything remotely attractive. We convince ourselves that the wee we've been in need of from the eye-wateringly strong coffee had in Puebla can wait until we get beyond Verín.

And we go to Xinzo de Limia, which, surely to goodness, has got to be better (but isn't, as you'll agree from what follows). We've still got one hundred and sixty kilometres to go to get to the outskirts of noisy, overcrowded, traffic-dominated Vigo, so we stop in Xinzo, coming off the A-52 onto a minor road. The need for that wee is becoming a necessity.

Surprisingly, we learn that Xinzo is home to more than ten thousand people. It's got a nationally famous glass factory, the obligatory service industries, and it's an area of general and varied agriculture. It's also one of the biggest producers of potatoes in the whole of Spain, to boot. Now there's a thing. It has few monuments of any interest whatsoever, as you might by now have guessed, but it does have a carnival which, the natives tell us, is the envy of a lot of people in this part of the world.

It's called the 'entroido' festival, the main character of which is the devil. Two or three of these devils, masked and in colourful costume and waving a threatening stick of some proportions, roam the streets at festival time in search of male denizens who are not correctly dressed in carnival clothes. These the devils solemnly cart off to the nearest bar to pay a fee for not being properly clothed for these jolly japes, and for not entering into the spirit of this exciting, not-to-be-missed event. Needless to say, the fine is a glass of wine.

So, Reader, next time you're at a loose end and you've had enough of the wonders of Salamanca and Segovia and Sevilla and others, haste ye at all speed to Xinzo de Limia to participate in this wonderful event, not to be missed (he repeats, with no small amount of sarcasm which he fails to control).

In conclusion, you'll ask yourself (and me!) why so many words have been lavished on ultra-modest Xinzo. There's only one reason: at the outset, I promised you a town or a city for every letter of the Spanish twenty-seven-lettered alphabet, and for better or worse it has to be Xinzo de Limia. Sorry about that, but there was little or no alternative.

Let's press on to 'Y', shall we?

26. Y for Yuste (eventually)

He was known in Spain and the far flung Spanish Empire as Charles
I of Spain. He was possibly more widely known as Charles V, the elected
(if such is the word) Emperor of the Holy Roman Empire. To those who
knew him on a daily, more intimate basis, he was known as Charles the
Greedy Get, though, for obvious reasons, such intimates chose not to
broadcast it in his presence, though he himself must have had some inkling,
faint though it might have been.

You see, Charles had what, over time, came to be known as a Habsburg jaw, the lower section of his face protruding more than is normally deemed natural. The logical outcome, unfortunately for him (and those of his clan), was that he had grave problems in chewing his food. This, in turn, brought about chronic indigestion, a great deal of flatulence at both ends, and a marked disinclination by those close to him to be close to him when he was at table. As a gourmet – or, a greedy get, if you want to put it that way – he ate prodigiously and adventurously, egging on his chefs to greater culinary efforts; but you get the impression, at this distant remove of centuries, that he didn't get any great lasting pleasure from eating. With age, gout got to him, rendering him chair-bound and bed-bound long before it did with men of his (comparative) age and disposition.

As to being King Charles of Spain, well, that was another problem. For a start, he wasn't actually born in Spain, could hardly speak Spanish (though he managed to get just beyond Principios Book I, eventually, never mastering the subjunctive), and he spent only sixteen of his forty years as king in his Spanish kingdom.

He was the eldest son of Juana I, the unfortunate Juana la Loca (Joan the Mad) and Flemish Philip the Handsome, whom poor Joan loved to bits, in spite of the fact that Phil had the most roving of roving eyes and indulged himself shamelessly in that direction. She even insisted on carting her husband's body all over Spain with her, unwilling to be convinced that he was dead, in spite of copious proof to the contrary.

Anyway, let's get back to Charles. He was brought up and educated in Flanders, with the result that when he was eventually declared King of Spain (his poor mother now judged to be as nutty as a fruitcake), he was to all intents and purposes a foreigner in his own kingdom. To make matters worse in his quest for acceptance in his adopted lands, he insisted on bringing with him, and placing in positions of considerable power and influence, a whole posse of his Flemish friends. As an example of his questionable choices, he appointed a sixteen year old Flemish youth Archbishop of Toledo, a position of immense wealth and power, the culmination of ecclesiastical achievement on earth (aside from the papacy, of course).

But in spite of his jaw and a ready inclination to pass audible and malodorous wind whilst eating, necessitating a frequent change of under-crackers, to say nothing of the fact that he must have felt a stranger in his own land, Charles was an ambitious bugger. When the position of Holy Roman Emperor became vacant, he diverted all his energies, to say nothing of an enormous amount of money, in his quest for this lofty position of earthly power. Those he couldn't threaten, he bought, ably assisted by the bottomless coffers of 'Them Fuggers', as they became known. Effectively, he mortgaged Spain to them.

At the time, Spain looked to be buoyant, knee deep in the gold plundered from the Americas, but this was, in time, to create a situation where financial ruin was just around the corner. An incidental corollary of this, of course, was that two civilisations, the Aztecs and the Incas, were wiped out in the pursuit of naked greed.

Not that everyone was chuffed with Charles' achievements, you understand, nor with the fact that his Empire and territories were well nigh beyond bounds: think 'Europe and Central and South America' and you'll not be far off. The French, as you might expect, now surrounded by Charles' possessions, were his mortal enemies, this time in the figure of Francis I. Frank and Charles simply detested each other. Charles suggested they settle their differences like real men, and issued the French king with the challenge of personal combat, winner takes all.

It never came to that, Francis being French and all that, as well as being a pompous prat (as was Charles, in his way), but they never became what you'd call chums, though they did learn, on an extremely basic level, to get along, in so far as that was politically possible. For all that, you have to admit the French had a case.

Charles' entire reign, all forty years of it, was taken up with war after war after war, and not just with the French, either. To maintain his position both at home – if you can call Spain his home – and abroad, he had to fight and threaten and bribe, which is a tiring existence, when you come to think about it. Not a lot's changed in politics, then, over the last four hundred years and more!

Protestantism clashed head on with Charles' entrenched, traditional Catholic outlook; the Turks and the Ottoman Empire were constantly snapping at his flanks, with the promise of more troubles as time went on; and he had problems galore with his own Kingdom of Spain.

In 1520, most of Castilla – by which terminology we probably mean 'the whole of Spain', Castilla being the essence of all things Spanish even then – was up in arms as Charles sought to impose his autocratic hand on an increasingly disgruntled nation, the nobility fearful for its future. Solution? He bought them off and still imposed his autocratic hand. The fact that during the Revolt of the Comuneros (Commoners) he had scores of his own subjects summarily executed seemed not to bother him over-much.

('Excuse me, I wonder if I might ask a question?'

'Well, can't it wait? I'm in full flow, don't you see?'

'Look, can you just clarify a little matter?'

'Which is?'

'I know we're near the end and you must be straining to get to the letter Z and all that, but I was just starting to wonder: this chapter is a history lesson, isn't it? Because, forgive the presumption, I thought this was an A to Z journey through Spain, and so far you've only mentioned

Flanders, which, by the way, is not in Spain.'

'I'm well aware of that, but just indulge me for a line or two more and all will be revealed, and you might just learn something to your advantage.'

'Hm.')

Where were we, now? Ah, Cheerful Charles the Glutton, king of all he surveyed, surrounded by supporters and sycophants and a multitude of enemies, seen and unseen, French and otherwise.

Well, the fact is that by 1555, in his middle fifties, and not what you'd call a well man, he woke up to yet another morning of wind-passing and indigestion and worsening gout, said to one and all – but mainly to himself – "Sod this for a game of soldiers", and promptly abdicated, leaving a dubious legacy to his son, who became Philip II of Armada fame.

('Look, Phil, I've got something of a surprise for you.'

'Oh?'

'Well, you know how you've been wanting to run your own ship, so to speak? Well, instead of a ship, I'm giving you the best part of the whole western world! How about that!'

'Oh, great! Just what I've always wanted!')

Which brings us nicely to the letter Y, the penultimate letter of the Spanish alphabet, and to Yuste. But before we get there with Charles – wait for it! – we'll follow him on his last journey south from Laredo in northern Cantabria, on beyond Reinosa of Blessed Memory, to distant, achingly beautiful Extremadura, his last pit-stop. And since his final earthly abode in Yuste wasn't yet readied to his remarkably humble expectations, he stopped off for three pleasant months in Jarandilla de la Vera, specifically in the Castle-Palace of the wealthy Counts of Oropesa.

Here, he ate prodigiously well, as he had done throughout his life, took in the views of this exceptionally picturesque western outpost of

Spain, wound down after a life of ambition and duplicity and political achievement, and got in a brickie to put a fireplace in his room. There, he waited on news from Yuste.

We four went to Yuste one bleak afternoon in March, 2010. We all knew Extremadura quite well: we'd been to Cáceres and Trujillo and Zafra, and even to traffic-jammed Mérida. On this particular occasion, we were based for a few nights in the wonderfully atmospheric parador of Navarredonda de Gredos, south-east of the city of Ávila, and very few kilometres from the Extremaduran border.

We went to find Jarandilla de la Vera – where, if you remember, Charles stayed for three very pleasant months, thank you very nicely – then on to Yuste, because, truth to tell, aside from Jarandilla's palace-parador and the jaw-dropping beauty of Extremadura's scenery, the small town of Jarandilla was doubling up as a morgue, seemingly, on the day we went there.

In Yuste, it was absolutely bucketing down. Spaniards say: 'it rained like big jars full'. There's an English description which fits the bill to perfection, but I'll withhold it in the interests of good breeding and a (rare) unwillingness to use profanity, however appropriate on this occasion. You might just know what I mean.

What you need to realise from the outset is that Yuste is the monastery and the monastery is Yuste, because, to all intents and purposes, there's nothing else in this neck of the woods (except fabulous scenery, of course). The monastery dates, originally, from the first years of the fifteenth century, though, as you might reasonably expect, little of the original survives in its pristine form in any significant way.

Apparently, two monks, keen to get even closer to God and further away from the temptations of life, left their hermitage in relatively close-by Plasencia and settled in these there hills. In the course of time, they were joined by other like-minded men of God, and settled on a piece of land donated by a local worthy who was sympathetic to their cause. Here they devoted their lives to prayer and physical hard, manual work, and their fame – of an ecclesiastical nature, you'll understand – spread, to the extent that by the early years of the century and shortly after their arrival, the congregation of monks was admitted into the Hieronymite Order. In time, the physical appearance of the monastery changed, parts demolished, parts adapted to the needs of the increasing number of monks and postulants: hospice, dormitories, refectory, gardens.

It attracted further donations and support from men of wealth and influence. Works of art were given or commissioned, artisans and painters and architects left their mark, and, by the time Charles and his retinue arrived, the Monastery of Saint Jerome at Yuste was established, its place in clerical circles assured. Its inhabitants, needless to say, had a significantly positive outcome for those living in the general area.

But, in all likelihood, if Charles had not chosen to end his days there, the monastery would undoubtedly have slipped into oblivion over the ensuing centuries, given its remote geographical situation and political fluctuations (most especially during the nineteenth century, if it were to last that long).

A dozen or so years before he upped sticks and left the world of political intrigue and fraud behind, Charles had expressed more than a passing interest in retiring, and, specifically, to Yuste. He'd been very clear, in various letters and documents, exactly what he wanted for his regal (though humble) apartments, which would effectively be tagged on to the existing monastery, allowing him easy access to the monastery itself; but he was at pains to stipulate that he would in no way interfere with the daily routine of the monks. In this, he kept his word.

Once there, with his fifty servants – twenty of whom worked in the kitchens on his behalf: let's not forget that Charles didn't stop being Charles the Greedy Get once he got religion – he settled down to an orderly life, and what he hoped would be a lengthy retirement. It turned out to be a stay of fewer than two years.

Apart from food, seemingly his number one priority, Charles indulged his passions for gardening (though there's no painting of him wielding shovel or hoe or similar gardening utensil), music, history, philosophy, geometry and – wait for it! – clocks. He was also keen to keep royal tabs on what was going on in his formerly owned dominions, and he was seldom without visits from people in high places.

But, for the king that he was and the king that he'd been, he lived fairly frugally, and his own quarters – which Alan inspected with his usual critical engineering eye, passing definitive judgement on things we three mere mortals were deemed to know little about – were modest. His living room and bedroom were simplicity itself, and they have been maintained wonderfully well to this day.

Which is fortuitous, since this wonderful building, redolent with history and boasting sublime architecture, went into a steady, very noticeable decline by the start of the nineteenth century. That French destroyer-in-chief, Napoleon Bonaparte, was responsible for setting fire to the monastery and royal apartments on a number of occasions during the invasion of Spain by his indisciplined troops. And later, some thirty years later, under the Secularisation Act of the brazenly anticlerical Mendizábal, the whole place was abandoned, and Nature took over, reducing much to rubble, though the basic construction was identifiable. Miguel de Unamuno – remember him from Salamanca? – expressed the view that 'even the ruins will perish'. He thought it 'a melancholy sight'.

(Mendizábal, by the way, was a Basque financial wizard, a violently anticlerical first minister, who closed all religious orders, their churches and convents and monasteries, since he thought, rightly, to an extent, that the Catholic Church had had it too good for too long. In an attempt to redistribute their lands and put them into the hands of the peasants, he confiscated Church lands – like Yuste – and put them up for sale. So far, a belting idea. Except for the fact that said peasants had no money to buy said lands, which were snapped up by people of wealth, thereby perpetuating an already unjust system which lasted well into the twentieth century, and was a significant cause of the Spanish Civil War. Some financial wizard, eh?)

Fortunately for everybody, and in spite of the monastery's appalling state, it was decreed in 1931 a 'monument of historical and artistic importance'. From then onwards, the only way was up, with the result that the miracle of the monastery's revival is now there for all to see and visit.

The pity is that when we were there, all ready to be impressed, we were so intent on not getting soaked to the skin by the unremitting downpour as we scrambled for every available space to take refuge, we most assuredly missed at least some parts of what it had to offer. Which, if you think about it, is a very good excuse, were any excuse needed, to go back and see it sometime very soon. Alan will be pleased: it'll give him an opportunity to explain his definitive thoughts at greater length. And perhaps it won't rain like big jars full next time.

(My own feeling is that the 'profanity' would have hit the nail on the head, but I've been over-ruled. Again. Some you win, some you lose.)

27. A difference of opinion(s)

I'm beginning to warm ever so slightly to Zamora. On the two dozen and more times that we'd driven from Madrid's Barajas airport the 600-plus kilometres up to Pontevedra (and back) we decided we needed to overnight somewhere nice, somewhere around the half way stage. Easyjet from Liverpool John Lennon didn't land in Madrid until around five in the afternoon, and the prospect of driving the almost 400 miles to Galicia was not one we relished. Especially in winter, with swirling mists and equally swirling snow (that once grounded us in Puebla de Sanabria, a lovely place to be grounded, by the way, in any sort of weather).

Zamora, geographically speaking, was something of a natural mid-point. For no reason I can explain, I also liked the name.

We'd been there before, of course, though first impressions were not entirely favourable. It just seemed like a large and expanding city with vistas of new flats and innumerable business parks, lots and lots of fairly anarchic traffic and under-passes and over-passes and zebra crossings and roundabouts. On top of this, we were put off by a little incident of no great merit in itself which we should have had the sense to dismiss, and didn't.

We'd stopped there for a couple of hours with a bus load of Pax Travel pilgrims (that wonderful lot from Runcorn, God bless them all, songs all the way there and back!) on our long way from Santiago de Compostela to Madrid, so we suggested they might want to see, at least, the cathedral, since we were ahead of time, and the idea of spending that time in an airport was not exactly to anybody's liking.

We walked them – strung out in an increasingly long line as they found things to see and buy and cafes and bars to stop and eat and drink in – up towards the cathedral, leaving the ever faithful Mariano with the coach in Calle de Vega, on the very edge of the monumental zone. Back in an hour, Mariano, unless we lose one of this lot (which is more than a distinct possibility!).

I asked the man on reception – face anything but remotely welcoming – if we could go in during the last half hour of its opening, before it closed at two o'clock. He told me, with complete disinterest, how much it cost: the ticket was, firstly, for the cathedral's museum, after which you gained automatic entry into the cathedral itself.

I explained to him nicely that we were Santiago pilgrims on our way back to Liverpool, that we were English Catholics of a strong persuasion who only wanted to go into the cathedral to say a prayer or two, to bring the pilgrimage to a fitting end (and maybe to say one for him, if we got a favourable reply). Face-like-a-smacked-arse shook his head wordlessly.

When I pressed him to be a little more forthcoming and to interpret the shaking head (which I increasingly felt like twatting with a pilgrim's staff), he told me rules were rules, and that if we wanted to see the inside of the cathedral – to pray, if you remember – we'd need to buy a ticket. I recall, very clearly, very strongly suggesting to him where he might shove all his tickets, not just ours, so as to bring severe and lasting pain to his rectum and a tear to his eye. I was pissed off on the grand scale with his attitude.

I know I've said it before elsewhere, and I make no apologies for repeating myself. I am a lover of most things Spanish (except for bullfights, which I can't abide, and octopus, the sight and smell of which turns my stomach), but I remain very far from impressed by state employees and their job-for-life, earning the easiest of livings in Spain's endlessly wonderful places of history and culture.

They are, almost without exception in my experience, unhelpful and condescending and frequently downright rude: the utterly stupid girl in wonderful Almagro's tiny tourist office who patently knew nothing of value about Barbara's Almagro; the ignorant dolly-birds in Burgos' magnificent Monasterio de Las Huelgas, who pointedly ignored the visitors, whilst keeping up a long, personal conversation with each other: "So I said to Mari Carmen why didn't she just ditch him and be done with it"; Beatriz from Burgos – and that's not her real name, by the way, to save what little is salvageable of her tattered reputation – grinding out her explanations, which she clearly didn't understand, in execrable English, and then pocketing one hundred and thirty euros for the ninety minute 'guided tour', happily choking on her cigarettes, walking thirty-odd English

Pax Travel pensioners into Burgos' oncoming traffic; and the clown in Santiago, whose English was incomprehensible, to the extent that I called a halt to the ninety minute guided tour after twenty minutes and was loudly applauded by Pax's pilgrims.

Add to them this state-employed specimen in Zamora and you might just sympathise with my not wanting to be associated with Zamora thereafter.

As if that weren't enough, Terrific Toro and Hotel Juan II are just up the road, so to speak, where generosity and outstanding service are the only acceptable norm.

But, ready to forgive and forget, and refusing to believe that Zamora had nothing worthy of our attention, I convinced a visibly reluctant Margaret to spend the second of our two day Toro visit in nearby Zamora.

And it's a very pleasant journey, both coming and going, comparatively flat by Spanish standards, with modest, sensuously undulating land and the odd sudden outcrops of plateau like giant bunkers on some giant golf course which Castilla's furiously bitter winter winds have yet to level.

Patches of mustard and orange and ochre and yellow and gold and brown and red. Vast fields of forty shades of green against the terra cotta coloured earth. A copse or two randomly scattered to indicate hidden springs and winding rivers hardly worthy of the name, never mentioned on any map. Gentle rises and barrelling lorries and spiralling, choking dust. Blue-on-white kilometre signs and red and white Avanza coaches. Solar panels by the thousands, as regular as soldiers on parade. Umbrella pines distantly looking all fluffy and touchable, and fields ploughed artistically at all angles. Cork trees, flat green against powder-lemon fields.

All very pretty, but it's eye-wateringly, bone-jarringly freezing in winter, preposterously hot in summer. Ask Laurie Lee: it nearly finished him in 1935, one year before the Spanish Civil War (of bitter memory).

So, here we are, positive and optimistic and ready to give Zamora our best shot, as they say. But where to start in this city of sixty thousand souls, two hundred and fifty kilometres north-west of Madrid, little more than sixty kilometres from Portugal's eastern border, bisected by the simply wonderful Antonio Machado's beloved River Duero.

There's only one real option for the first sight, the cathedral, and it lies in that very small cultural and monumental section of the city in its south-west corner, huddled like a little redoubt against encroaching modernity.

Like most things architectural, your appreciation of a cathedral is an entirely personal, subjective one. I won't say that the interior is disappointing, but its exterior is undeniably its best feature: a 'sturdy pile', The Book says, topped off, literally, by its comparatively riotous dome of Byzantine inspiration.

When Arse Face is on duty – and I saw him again, though he didn't recognise me on this occasion – you'll enter via the museum, wend your way around the cloisters, then into the cathedral proper, started in the twelfth century, with all its different chapels, 'sponsored' by the rich and powerful of long ago as a passport to Eternal Life. Large areas of the internal walls are actually painted murals, as most medieval cathedrals once were, by the way.

Inside, you'll be struck by how unexpectedly small the cathedral is: not much bigger than two tennis courts side by side.

The cathedral's nave is almost totally taken up by the choir, the work of one John of Brussels, one of the many highly qualified itinerant jobbers who abounded throughout the length and breadth of medieval Spain. Gil de Siloe (and other members of his numerous tribe) was another to leave his mark on Castilla's cathedrals and churches and monasteries.

It's a matter of opinion, I suppose, but to these eyes John got it all wrong, because unless you actually go around its bulk in search of the High Altar, you'll never see what is surely the focal point of any cathedral. Both the choir's size and position basically minimise the impact of the cathedral and effectively exclude those congregated behind it from any real participation in the cathedral's ceremonies. Its position, both here and in many of Spain's cathedrals, seems somehow to dehumanise the whole building.

In León's cathedral, with its choir similarly located, they got around this problem in recent times by 'opening up' the back wall of the choir, encasing it with enormous glass doors. The effect is simply startling and immediately welcoming, and you can see everything and feel a part of the whole. Maybe other cathedrals might consider this simple change for the better, which in no way spoils the cathedral's heritage.

By Spanish standards – which are frequently over the top for the more sober British visitors: take Burgos, for example – Zamora's marble altar piece, the 'retablo' of The Transfiguration, is remarkably conservative. Added some six centuries after the cathedral was first started, it seems, for all its sobriety, rather at odds with the rest of the building.

In its way, the cathedral is nice – he said, damning it with faint praise – but it didn't inspire me to prayer, contemplation or excessive admiration. Mind you, I have to confess that I was desperate for a coffee, and that might have minimally coloured my judgement. But only minimally.

You come out of the cathedral via the Portada del Obispo. Literally steps from the gate is the bishop's palace, so getting to work was never likely to provide him with a problem, bless him and his little red silk socks. And if you turn right after the official residence and slip down the slope of Peñas de Santa Marta, you'll be able to see the broad Duero on its way to the distant Atlantic via Portuguese Oporto.

Now go back the short distance to the square in front of the cathedral as far as Rua de los Notarios, onwards along the Rua de Francos and Rua de Ramón Carrión. This whole four hundred metre stretch, ending in the Main Square, is endowed left and right with a number of exceptional Romanesque churches and other religious monuments, no fewer than twenty-two of the latter in the sixty-three monuments mentioned in the city's official brochure.

There's the Churches of San Isidro, San Claudio de Olivares, Santiago de Los Caballeros, San Pedro and San Ildefonso, La Magdalena, Santa María La Nueva, San Cipriano, Santo Tomé. Shall I go on? No? Fair enough: you've got the idea.

The Main Square, anything but a regular shape, and very ordinary when compared to such as Salamanca and Madrid, nevertheless makes you smile as you look around, built on a tilting plateau that appears to edge ever so gently in search of the Duero. And almost in the centre of the square is the Romanesque church of San Juan de la Puerta Nueva.

Apart from this attractive section of the city, barely one tenth of what we might call Greater Zamora, little remains of Zamora's past as an important, strategic frontier town, with Portugal almost in sight to the west. The city was situated on the famous Roman Vía de la Plata, The Silver Road, and during the lengthy period of La Reconquista (The Reconquest) – more than seven centuries off and on: more off than on, it has to be said, as Christian kings and nobles squabbled and fought each other for personal gain instead of uniting definitively to expel the infidel – the town was fiercely contested by opposing armies.

Modern Zamora has hugely expanded beyond its original boundaries, very much like Ávila and Palencia, but its 'casco histórico' still deservedly draws praise and admiration and visitors.

Margaret's still not entirely convinced, but it's true to say that she's got to the heady heights of lukewarm where Zamora is concerned, and I suppose that's progress of a sort, and Zamora will be pleased with this (limited) praise from an exacting Hispanist. That said, she's let it be known she won't be going back any day soon, so there.

(Post Script: I once asked Manuel, my headmaster-student and an experienced world traveller, what he thought of the city. "Nothing special", was his pithy reply. Yet The Lovely Ana Lobato from Puebla quite likes it. So go and see for yourself and make up your own mind, Reader.)

(Post Post Script: 'Rome wasn't built in a day' is rendered in Spanish by the expression: 'No se ganó Zamora en una hora'. Something more for your edification, Reader.)